BEND YOUR
BRAIN

BEND YOUR
BRAIN

151 PUZZLES, TIPS, AND TRICKS TO BLOW (AND GROW) YOUR MIND

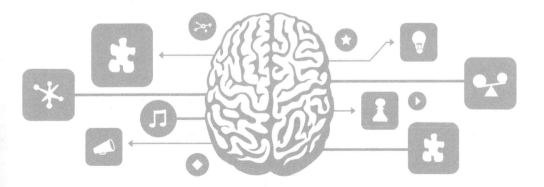

THREE RIVERS PRESS • NEW YORK

Published in the United States by Three Rivers Press, an imprint of the Crown Publishing Group, a division of Random House LLC, a Penguin Random House Company, New York.
www.crownpublishing.com

THREE RIVERS PRESS and the Tugboat design are registered trademarks of Random House LLC.

Library of Congress Cataloging-in-Publication Data has been applied for.

ISBN 978-0-8041-4009-6

Printed in the United States of America

Book design by Marbles: The Brain Store
Illustrations by Angie Brown and Nicole Willer
Cover design by Marbles: The Brain Store

10 9 8 7 6 5 4 3 2 1

First Edition

INTRODUCTIONS

What Marbles Is 7

What Your Brain Is 8

What This Book Is 9

PUZZLES

Visual Perception 14

Word Skills 44

Critical Thinking 74

Coordination 106

Memory 136

CONCLUSIONS

For Those Who Still Have Questions 168

For Those Interested in Who the Puzzlers Are 189

WELCOME

Before you get started,
here are just a few pages of information to
officially introduce you to the ideas behind this book:

your brain

MEET

marbles®
the brain store

what we are

Marbles: The Brain Store is a first-of-its-kind shop offering handpicked, expert-tested, fun-filled products to strengthen your brain.

what we do

we build
BETTER BRAINS

how we do it

We use five brain-building, scientifically validated categories to help you discover how to unlock all the areas of your brain:

VISUAL PERCEPTION	WORD SKILLS	CRITICAL THINKING	COORDI-NATION	MEMORY

your brain

MEET

your brain

what it is

This master organ, weighing in at approximately three pounds, controls all the systems of your body—giving you the ability to:

MOVE + FEEL EMOTION + STORE MEMORIES + COMMUNICATE + HAVE A PERSONALITY

(all of this—and more—through a network of billions of nerve cells!)

where it is

There are five major parts (regions) that make up your powerful human mind:

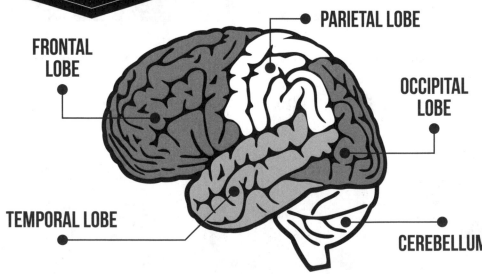

PARIETAL LOBE

FRONTAL LOBE

OCCIPITAL LOBE

TEMPORAL LOBE

CEREBELLUM

MEET

your brain

BEND YOUR **BRAIN**

---

why be here

Breakthrough research has shown that you can generate new brain cells as you use your brain to focus, create, and play!

➡ **YOU LOVE PUZZLES!**

➡ **YOU LOVE YOUR BRAIN!**

---

why this book

To give your brain a well-rounded workout that's structured around these three brain-health facts:

① Use it or lose it!

Thanks to neuroplasticity, your brain can form new cells and new connections at any age. So there's no excuse to stop building your brain!

② Variety is good.

As with all muscles, working one more than others will just leave you lopsided. Keep your synapses strong by training all the different areas of your brain!

③ Be specific.

Finding your keys is the least of your worries if you can't remember where you parked the car. So if you need to build a certain part of your brain, do it.

 your brain

MEET

what it is

Each section of the book is divided into five levels of difficulty (distinguished in the top outermost corner of each page). This is because:

> **"WHEN YOU DO SOMETHING OVER AND OVER AGAIN, GRADUALLY INCREASING THE DIFFICULTY, THAT'S HOW YOU GET MAJOR BRAIN CHANGE!"**

MIND=WARMING

1

These puzzles are the easiest and a great place for beginners to start.

MIND=STRETCHING

2

These puzzles are all about getting your brain moving and shaking.

MIND=GROWING **③**

These puzzles take your brain out of its comfort zone to inspire growth.

MIND=BURSTING **④**

These puzzles are intended to directly challenge your brain.

MIND=BLOWING **⑤**

These puzzles are meant to be difficult. Most will take a few minutes to solve, some may take hours, but all will cause some major brain changes and development!

 BRAIN FACT: Along the way, you will often discover a brain fact, tip, or trick in a section that looks like this. Sometimes it will tell you how a puzzle is working your brain; sometimes it will blow your mind.

(deep breath)

LET THE
BRAIN
BUILDING
BEGIN →

VISUAL PERCEPTION

BASED IN THE OCCIPITAL LOBE

Information taken in through the eyes is perceived and analyzed to allow for tasks like walking or driving.

WHAT IT DOES

As a combined function of both our eyes and brain, visual perception allows you to see images as a whole rather than broken down into visual elements.

 = + + + + +

HOW IT WORKS

Shifting an object's orientation in your mind or recognizing an object's shape and color produces four major visual processes:

      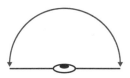   

VISUAL MEMORY

Ability to retrieve visual images and/or experiences

PERIPHERAL VISION

Ability to view objects that occur outside the very center of gaze

USEFUL FIELD OF VIEW

Ability to extract information within a visual area with a brief glance

DIVIDED ATTENTION

Ability to successfully execute more than one action at a time

PUZZLE #1: WORDIES

A typographical quandary: If a picture is worth a thousand words, what does a picture of words go for? In this game, pictures are used to represent a word or phrase. Note: The word placement within the frame is important.

HERE ARE SOME EXAMPLES TO GET YOU STARTED:

BoPUSSots	EASY PIECES EASY PIECES EASY PIECES EASY PIECES EASY PIECES	SCHOOL

The word "PUSS" is in the word "BOOTS," so the answer is "Puss in Boots."

The phrase "EASY PIECES" appears five times, so the answer is "Five Easy Pieces."

The word "SCHOOL" is high in the box, so the answer is "High School."

a

theflyointment

ANSWERS:

b

OATH
lying

c

PUT
WEIGHT

d

LipLip

PUZZLE #2: UNTAGGED TOURIST

Long ago in a time of yore, photos were not digitally dated or tagged with their location when the snapshot was made. Instead, folk had to label their photos by hand. Dark times. Below are eight such untagged photos. Can you tell which state they were taken in?

(Petri Krohn at the English language Wikipedia)

(Raime via Wikimedia Commons)

ANSWERS:

(Tim Pearce, Los Gatos, via Wikimedia Commons)

(Some rights reserved by RNHurt)

(Rdikeman at the English language Wikipedia)

(Rennett Stowe from USA via Wikimedia Commons)

PUZZLE #3: VIZWORDS

Set aside your knowledge of suffixes and prefixes—today, we make words of pictures! Can you put one picture together with one word part to create a complete word related to food? Note: Each picture and word part may be used only once. Spelling may not always be correct, but pronunciation will be.

FOR EXAMPLE:

+ NA

The picture shows the number "2" and the word part is "NA," so the answer is "Tuna."

(Zedcor Wholly Owned/PhotoObjects.net/Thinkstock)

(Valua Vitaly/iStock/Thinkstock)

(Maridav/iStock/Thinkstock)

(Jan Sandvik/iStock/Thinkstock)

(Jupiterimages/Photos.com/Thinkstock)

BO	TARINE	CHES
BAGE	KIN	BROW

ANSWERS:

PUZZLE #4: WORDIES

Typographical quandary #2: If the pen is mightier than the sword, where does that put the keyboard? In this game, pictures are used to represent a word or phrase. Note: The word placement within the frame is important.

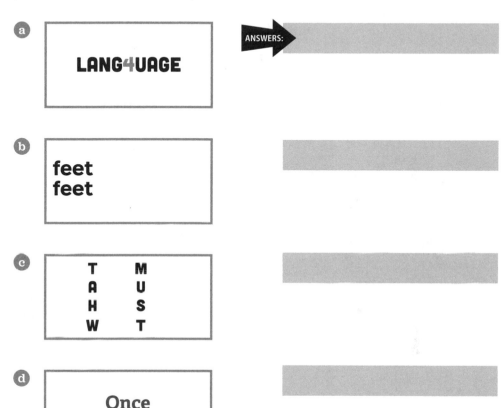

a

LANG4UAGE

ANSWERS:

b

feet
feet

c

T   M
A   U
H   S
W   T

d

Once
11:37 PM

....

 **BRAIN FACT:** The above puzzle requires attention to the spatial placement of the words. Your ability to see the spatial relationships between objects (scientists call this an allocentric frame of reference) is dependent on the ventral visual processing stream, which runs from the back of the brain (primary visual cortex) along the bottom of the cortex through the temporal lobe.

PUZZLE #5: COMPOUND IT!

Everyone knows that two heads are better than one, so only slightly questionable logic maintains that two words together should also be magical. Can you pair up the twelve images below in order to make six compound words?

FOR EXAMPLE:

The pictures show: a stick of BUTTER and a FLY, so the answer is "Butterfly."

(Stockbyte/Stockbyte/Thinkstock)   (Dimijana/iStock/Thinkstock)

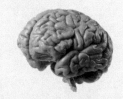

(Stephen Kirklys/iStock/Thinkstock)

(Barbara DudziÀska/iStock/Thinkstock)

(Xavier Perez/iStock/Thinkstock)

(Purestock/Thinkstock)

(miketanct/iStock/Thinkstock)

(Digital Vision./Digital Vision/Thinkstock)

(gualbertobecerra/iStock/Thinkstock)

(IvanMikhaylov/iStock/Thinkstock)

(Nastco/iStock/Thinkstock)

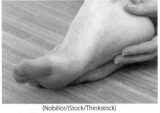

(Nobilior/iStock/Thinkstock)

(Burke/Triolo Productions/Stockbyte/Thinkstock)

(Cheryl Davis/iStock/Thinkstock)

ANSWERS:

PUZZLE #6: WORDIES

Typographical point of interest: Thinking outside the box isn't always the best way to go about things. Sometimes a good box isn't a bad thing. In this game, pictures are used to represent a word or phrase. Note: The word placement within the frame is important.

a

s e b l s g i n s

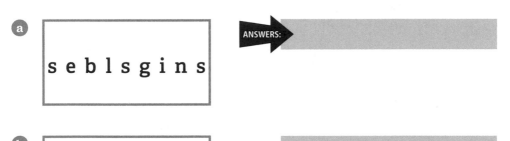
ANSWERS:

b

**your hat
keep it**

c

**I HAVE
_DEA**

d

BAN   ANA

BRAIN FACT: Maybe the best way to solve the puzzle above is to "think outside the box" while thinking inside the box. Creativity often benefits from constraints. For example, studies have found that people are more creative after reading or thinking about something absurd or paradoxical.

PUZZLE #7: COMMON BONDS

Relationships between things can be subtle. For example, a common thread among three things could be as easy as a spoken word or different spelling, or...

HERE IS AN EXAMPLE TO GET YOU STARTED:

GAME A

The pictures show: a SATURN dealership, the element MERCURY, and a statue of NEPTUNE, so the answer is "Planets."

ANSWERS:

... as complex as rocket surgery. With that in mind, can you find the common bond among the very different pictures in the games below?

GAME B

(tasken/iStock/Thinkstock)

(david Fanklin/iStock/Thinkstock)

(Andy Dean/Hemera/Thinkstock)

GAME C

(metrjohn/iStock/Thinkstock)

(wrangel/iStock/Thinkstock)

(eric Isselee/iStock/Thinkstock)

PUZZLE #8: IDENTIFY THE MASCOT

Lots of companies use human, or nearly human, mascots to identify their brand. Can you identify these common mascots? Or, rather, the name of the company each mascot represents? (Bonus points if you can give the name of the mascot too!)

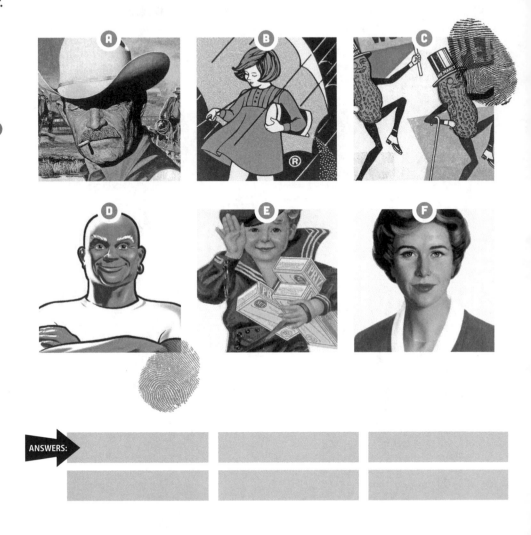

ANSWERS:

....

🧠 **BRAIN FACT:** Personification (i.e., signifying something by way of a memorable character or personality) is a marketing technique that makes use of the halo effect. The mascot or character is given certain . . .

... positive qualities that, almost like a halo, also surround the product itself. This halo effect works with people too. When someone is rated as more attractive, they also tend to be rated as being more intelligent, more ethical, more friendly, etc.

PUZZLE #9: VIZWORDS

Have you ever repeated a word over and over until it seemed to lose meaning? Don't do that with this puzzle. Instead, make nine words related to a geographical place out of one picture and one word part. Each picture and word part will be used only once.

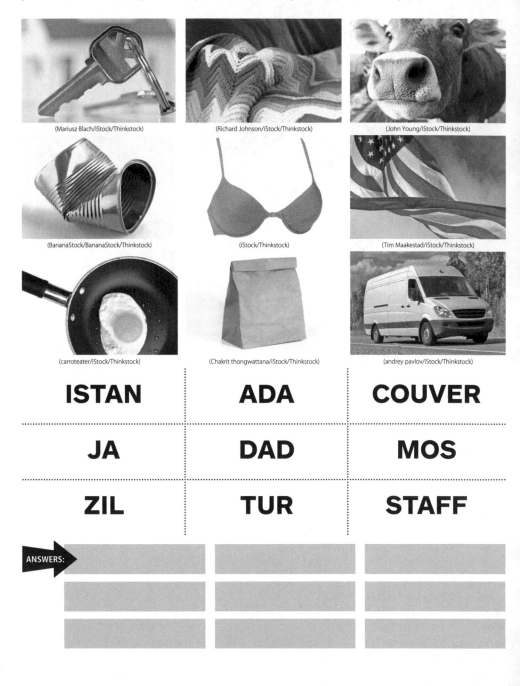

(Mariusz Blach/iStock/Thinkstock)

(Richard Johnson/iStock/Thinkstock)

(John Young/iStock/Thinkstock)

(BananaStock/BananaStock/Thinkstock)

(iStock/Thinkstock)

(Tim Maakestad/iStock/Thinkstock)

(carroteater/iStock/Thinkstock)

(Chakrit thongwattana/iStock/Thinkstock)

(andrey pavlov/iStock/Thinkstock)

ISTAN	ADA	COUVER
JA	DAD	MOS
ZIL	TUR	STAFF

ANSWERS:

PUZZLE #10: WORDIES

The final typographical quandary (for this book, anyway): What kind of font would one use for the writing on the walls? In this game, pictures are used to represent a word or phrase. Note: The word placement within the frame is important.

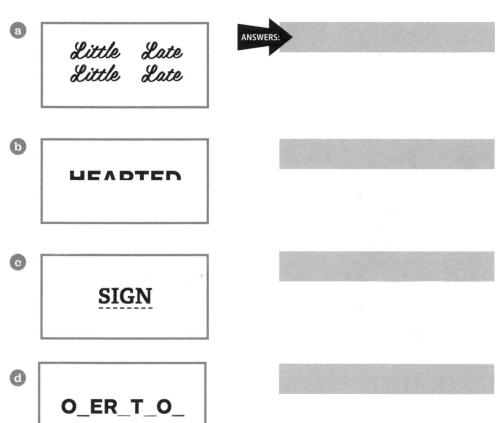

(a)

Little   Late
Little   Late

ANSWERS:

(b)

HEARTED

(c)

SIGN

(d)

O_ER_T_O_

....

 **BRAIN FACT:** The part of your brain responsible for processing the meaning of words is called Wernicke's area. Damage to this area can result in fluent aphasia, a condition where people can say words, often very confidently, but what comes out is typically nonsense.

PUZZLE #11: VIZWORDS

Words can sometimes work like music—if you put specific sounds together, they might create a thing of beauty and insight. For this puzzle, can you put together one picture with one word part to create a complete word? Each picture and word part will be used once.

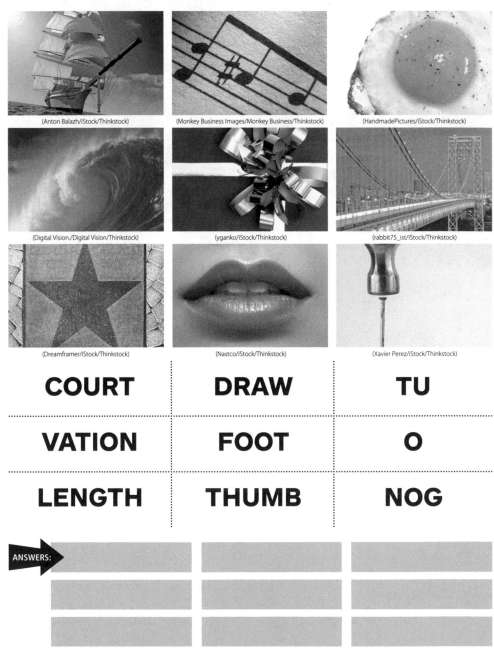

(Anton Balazh/iStock/Thinkstock)

(Monkey Business Images/Monkey Business/Thinkstock)

(HandmadePictures/iStock/Thinkstock)

(Digital Vision./Digital Vision/Thinkstock)

(yganko/iStock/Thinkstock)

(rabbit75_ist/iStock/Thinkstock)

(Dreamframer/iStock/Thinkstock)

(Nastco/iStock/Thinkstock)

(Xavier Perez/iStock/Thinkstock)

COURT	DRAW	TU
VATION	FOOT	O
LENGTH	THUMB	NOG

ANSWERS:

PUZZLE #12: COMPOUND IT!

As a loose analogy, a family of words would be a sentence, and a village of words a paragraph. So a compound word must be two best friends. Can you pair up the twelve images below in order to make six two-word phrases or compound words (i.e., a word that is made up of two words, such as "butterfly")? Each image will be used only once.

(david franklin/iStock/Thinkstock)

(Lyudmila Suvorova/iStock/Thinkstock)

(miflippo/iStock/Thinkstock)

(Spencer Berger/iStock/Thinkstock)

(Ingram Publishing/Thinkstock)

(Sebalos/Thinkstock)

(Dave King/Thinkstock)

(Iwona Grodzka/iStock/Thinkstock)

(slav/iStock/Thinkstock)

(Evgeny Karandaev/iStock/Thinkstock)

(Vitali Dyatchenko/iStock/Thinkstock)

(robeo/iStock/Thinkstock)

ANSWERS:

PUZZLE #13: COMMON BONDS

Finding similarities among things sometimes just requires a closer look. For biologists, that means a microscope. For detectives, a magnifying glass. For this puzzle . . .

GAME A	GAME B

(an2002/iStock/Thinkstock)
(Juanmonino/iStock/Thinkstock)
(suesmith2/iStock/Thinkstock)
(Azurita/iStock/Thinkstock)

ANSWERS:

. . . just your eyes. Can you find the common bond among the very different pictures in the games below?

GAME C

GAME D

(Tomwang112/iStock/Thinkstock)

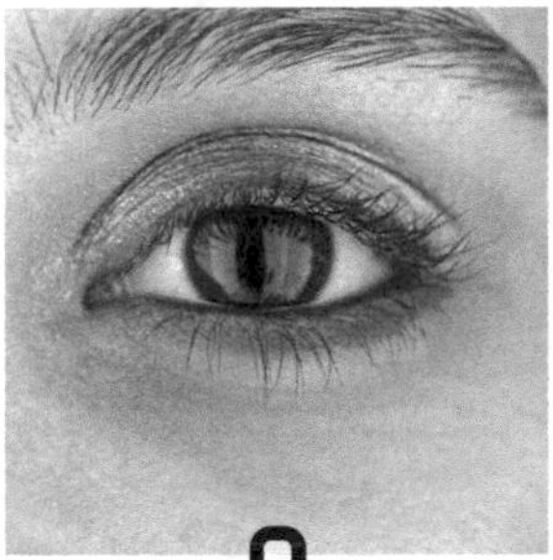

(Creatas Images/Creatas/Thinkstock)

(mflippo/iStock/Thinkstock)

(Chris Elwell/iStock/Thinkstock)

(Photo by Alan Light)

(Michał Różewski/iStock/Thinkstock)

PUZZLE #14: VIZWORDS

Technically, every word is a chain of little pictures. Think about it. For this next puzzle, can you put one picture together with one word part to create a complete word related to jobs? Each picture and word part will be used only once.

(Antonio_Diaz/iStock/Thinkstock)

(Mariusz Blach/iStock/Thinkstock)

(Valentyn Volkov/iStock/Thinkstock)

(Maciej Maksymowicz/iStock/Thinkstock)

(litu92458/iStock/Thinkstock)

(Burke/Triolo Productions/Stockbyte/Thinkstock)

(Bob Ingelhart/iStock/Thinkstock)

(zveiger alexandre/iStock/Thinkstock)

BER	LOT	IST
FIRE	ACIST	PENTER
MITH	JOC	CHER

ANSWERS:

PUZZLE #15: VISUAL ODD MAN OUT

Like a bull in a china shop, some things don't belong. Three of the four pictures in each puzzle below are related in some way and one is not. Can you find and circle the picture that doesn't belong?

GAME A

A

B

C

D

(Photofest)

GAME B

A

B

C

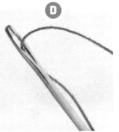
D

(Jupiterimages/Creatas/Thinkstock) (Hemera Technologies/Photos.com/Thinkstock) (iStock) (Marcco73/iStock/Thinkstock)

GAME C

A

B

C

D

(vah-dee/iStock/Thinkstock) (Stockbyte/Stockbyte/Thinkstock) (Jens Gade/iStock/Thinkstock)

GAME D

A

B

C

D

(Gage Skidmore) (Photofest)

PUZZLE #16: COMPOUND IT!

Some pairs are so great that they have to be stacked together. Like "dragonfly" and "skyscraper," the words just work better together. Can you pair up the twelve images below in order to make six two-word phrases or compound words (i.e., a word that is made up of two words, such as "butterfly")? Each image will be used only once.

(Miles Higgins/iStock/Thinkstock)

(Danny Smythe/iStock/Thinkstock)

(BrianAJackson/iStock/Thinkstock)

(Ryan Warnick/iStock/Thinkstock)

(Robert Marfin/iStock/Thinkstock)

(Irina Tischenko/iStock/Thinkstock)

(pressureUA/iStock/Thinkstock)

(Dreamframer/iStock/Thinkstock)

(Stockbyte/Stockbyte/Thinkstock)

(alkir/iStock/Thinkstock)

(Jorgen Udvang/iStock/Thinkstock)

ANSWERS:

PUZZLE #17: REBUS

Rebuses have been around for hundreds of years. They are visual games that use pictures to represent words or parts of words in a phrase or sentence. (And while they don't require calculus to find the sum of their parts, that doesn't mean they're easy!)

FOR EXAMPLE:

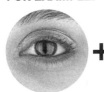 + [glove] − G + U

This rebus is translated as EYE + LOVE (Glove minus the G) + U—or, I love you.

[bee] + 4 + GOD + [spider web/spider] − B +

R + [brick wall] − W + E + [quilt] − T +

E + *yyy* + [hand] − H + E + [quilt] −

T + E + [jester] + ISH.

(Creatas Images/Creatas/Thinkstock)
(claudiodivizia, Pavel Lebedinsky, tassel78, worac, Eric R. Perlstrom, and canmocan/iStock/Thinkstock)
(Ablestock.com/ Ablestock.com/Thinkstock)

 hint!

 → ALBERT EINSTEIN SAID IT.

PUZZLE #18: COMPOUND IT!

Can you pair up the twelve images below in order to make six two-word phrases or compound words (i.e., a word that is made up of two words, such as "butterfly")? Each image will be used only once.

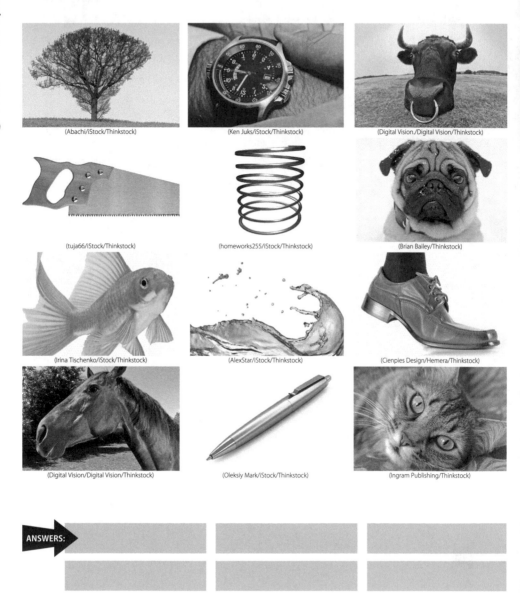

(Abachi/iStock/Thinkstock)

(Ken Juks/iStock/Thinkstock)

(Digital Vision./Digital Vision/Thinkstock)

(tuja66/iStock/Thinkstock)

(homeworks255/iStock/Thinkstock)

(Brian Bailey/Thinkstock)

(Irina Tischenko/iStock/Thinkstock)

(AlexStar/iStock/Thinkstock)

(Cienpies Design/Hemera/Thinkstock)

(Digital Vision/Digital Vision/Thinkstock)

(Oleksiy Mark/iStock/Thinkstock)

(Ingram Publishing/Thinkstock)

ANSWERS:

PUZZLE #19: COVER LETTER

Find and colorize the words that begin with the letter "L." Some pictures may be repeated more than once. (And feel free to use your brightest colors here!) Hint: There are 20 items.

 **BRAIN FACT:** Object shapes are processed in the lateral occipital complex. Neurons in this area do not respond to the individual lines or orientation of a shape, but rather to the shape as a whole.

PUZZLE #20: WHOSE MOUTH IS IT?

They say that our eyes are windows to our soul, but can you identify these famous ladies by just their mouths?

a

(Photofest)

ANSWERS:

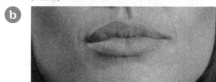

b

(Photofest)

c

(Photofest)

hint!
HER MOTTO IS "NO PAIN, NO GAIN."

d

(Photofest)

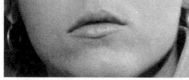

e

(Photofest)

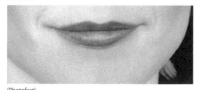

f

(Photofest)

hint!
HER COOKBOOK IS "ALL GOOD."

 BRAIN FACT: You have a brain region in the temporal lobe that selectively processes faces. It is called FFA, which stands for Fantabulous Face Area. Just kidding, it stands for fusiform face area.

PUZZLE #21: REBUS

Rebuses have been around for hundreds of years. They are visual games that use pictures to represent words or parts of words in a phrase or sentence. If it helps you solve the puzzle, think of them like charades, only on paper.

QUI + − +

 + PLE + H + − C +

THE + − C + EST

+ M + $9\tfrac{9}{99}$ − N.

ANSWER:

(Hemera Technologies/Photos.com/Thinkstock)
(Tony Campbell, Chris Elwell, Eric Isselée, and Silent47/iStock/Thinkstock)

hint!

→ STEPHEN HAWKING SAID IT.

PUZZLE #22: COVER LETTER

Find and colorize the words that begin with the letter "R." Some pictures may be repeated more than once. (Also, feel free to get creative and try coloring with rosy tones or practice your cross-hatching here!) Hint: There are 35 items in total, and once you've found them all, something you've been looking for will be revealed.

PUZZLE #23: WHOSE MOUTH IS IT?

They say that our eyes are windows to our soul, but can you identify these famous gentlemen by just their mouths?

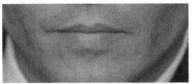

(Photofest)

ANSWERS:
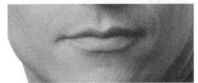

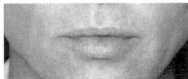

(Photofest)

hint!
THIS PUZZLE MAKES HIS RIDICULIST.

(Photofest)

(Photofest)

(Photofest)

hint! HIS LIFE GOT FLIPPED
TURNED UPSIDE DOWN.

(Photofest)

BRAIN FACT: When your FFA is damaged, it often results in a disorder called prosopagnosia—the inability to see faces! People with this disorder can still see shapes, colors, and textures, but never faces.

41

PUZZLE #24: REBUS

Rebuses have been around for hundreds of years. They are visual games that use pictures to represent words or parts of words in a phrase or sentence.

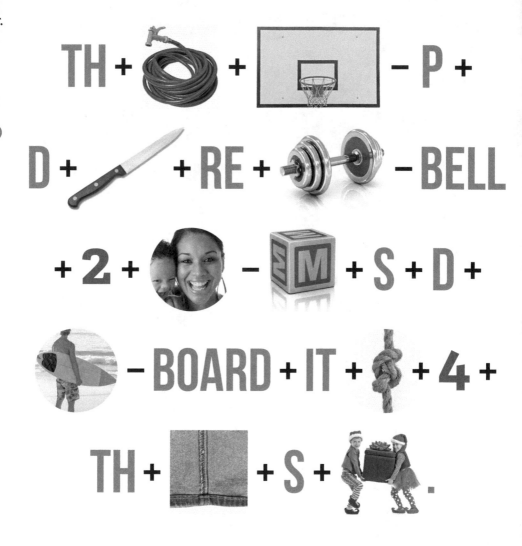

ANSWER:

 hint!

→ **ABRAHAM LINCOLN SAID IT.**

PUZZLE #25: FIND THE ANACHRONISMS

Pictured below are some old-fashioned objects that would have existed in normal American life from 1861–1865. Also pictured below are some anachronisms, or things that are chronologically inconsistent.

visual
perception
MASTER

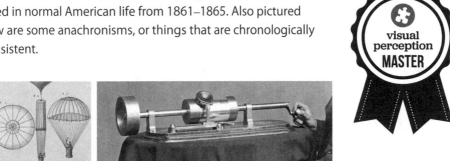

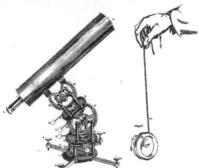

WORD SKILLS

BASED IN THE PARIETAL LOBE

Word skills give you an understanding of language's structure and how to best express yourself—whether listening, speaking, reading, or writing.

WHAT THEY DO

They improve your vocabulary (by relating new words with words you already know), stimulate your creativity, help you recognize letter patterns, and make it easier to learn new languages.

ABC

HOW THEY WORK

Word skills are an example of an "association area" because they use multiple types of input from all your lobes—allowing you to process information from all your senses.

I SEE...   I FEEL...   I TASTE...   I SMELL...   I HEAR...

PUZZLE #1: CAROUSEL

Find adjoining words to make one complete clockwise path all the way around the word-find grid so that you **ONLY USE FOUR-LETTER WORDS** and **EVERY WORD STARTS WITH THE LAST LETTER OF THE PREVIOUS WORD.**

FEEL FREE TO CUT SOME CORNERS TO FINISH THIS PUZZLE.

```
        T O R E P
      S Z X N E S T
    H K J O K W R M F
    T J I O D O U N U O I
    B U R N X H E V E N O K L
  B H Y R J S Y   H Y G E T I N
  U J O V U O       E K V X A A
  N T A E N           T G Y T E
  T E L L I E       U L F E N D
  G I G S U N A   N H I N V K H
    E V E R D R A R U T O O L
    L E X S U Z A Z A H U
      B E R K Y P A L G
        A J O N O I L
          Y V Y E S
```

a

Find adjoining words to make one complete clockwise path all the way around the word-find grid so that you **ONLY USE ONE-SYLLABLE WORDS** and **EVERY WORD STARTS WITH THE LAST LETTER OF THE PREVIOUS WORD.**

```
        B U E G H
      I T T H Q M T
    L V U S O G I F A
    K G J R V N N Z D S R
    N R V M X I K E B F M A C
  M H C S S A P   H L L A M W J
  G W B R F O       Q D Y P I G
  A E N M L           U F O L P
  I S A F J N       J H T K C F
  K T U L X I G   W N M L E B Z
    O R E K O N E S O J Q U R
    P S T E N G U K I L W
      Q S B I N D E T H
        A P T U Y L S
          F H O K C
```

b

PUZZLE #2: CAROUSEL

Find adjoining words to make one complete clockwise path all the way around the word-find grid so that you **ONLY USE WORDS WITH DOUBLE LETTERS** and **EVERY WORD STARTS WITH THE LAST LETTER OF THE PREVIOUS WORD.**

THIS SEEMS LIKE ONE OF THOSE TIMES WORKING IN CIRCLES WILL BE USEFUL.

```
        A W O O C
      L C Y N J O F
      L I D H E D G G T
    T O D A V X L B O U K
  T J E E N K M I L A T T E
  B S S V L O B   Q X C Y R G G
  N X Z N O L       W Z R Q K K
  N O O N S           O F T S A
  F O E J R P         R I D D L E
  H E O M L E P   A I Z D U N P
  R U L L I R H T C Z K D M
    B O Z K D P O P F L H
      B T B K S O M E Y
        V D W R C S K
          G A A S Y
```

(a)

Find adjoining words to make one complete clockwise path all the way around the word-find grid so that you **ONLY USE ACTION WORDS** and **EVERY WORD STARTS WITH THE LAST LETTER OF THE PREVIOUS WORD.**

```
          C R G J N
        L T W L I H C
        D F R E T N E V O
      S F T Y M Q U F C P Y
    N U D H J U B G T R T E B
  S H S I W T O   V S O F O A C
  A T G O O U       H K R M S H
  F S D M R           R Z D H P
  K I R K H Z         I L P O U F
  P I L O T W P   L E W U T K M
    A D S L D S J L R N Q E G
    Y V N L L E W D O X V
    V Y Q E R S N L B
      N P O A K J P
        E V I D W
```

(b)

PUZZLE #3: CAROUSEL

Find adjoining words to make one complete clockwise path all the way around the word-find grid so that you **ONLY USE TWO-SYLLABLE WORDS** and **EVERY WORD STARTS WITH THE LAST LETTER OF THE PREVIOUS WORD.**

Find adjoining words to make one complete clockwise path all the way around the word-find grid so that you **ONLY USE FIVE-LETTER WORDS** and **EVERY WORD STARTS WITH THE LAST LETTER OF THE PREVIOUS WORD.**

IF A CIRCUS AND A WORD SEARCH GOT TOGETHER, THIS WOULD BE THE MAIN ATTRACTION!

PUZZLE #4: PHRASE FINDER

These next few puzzles are for fans of the good ol' word search, just with a little more oomph. Or moxy. Your choice. Find the words hidden in the word search that will help you to fill in the boxes and complete the common phrase. The words may be forward, backward, or diagonal.

ⓐ

```
W T K V T C U H
L A U G H I N G
R Y Y L E K K E
D P L Z N N F H
S A C A X O N T
L H B Y T I L P
```

Row 1: _ _ _ **G** _ _ _ _ **A** _ _
Row 2: _ _ **E** _ _ **Y** _ **T** _ _
Row 3: _ _ **H** _ _ _ **N** _

ⓑ

DOES THIS MEAN YOU SHOULD ONLY GET GOLD FILLINGS?

```
J W O Y N F Y O
Y M H K C I M H
H O B E P S R T
F N U V R U N U
T E X R O E T O
W Y S Y L P R M
```

Row 1: _ **P** _ _ **O** _ _ _
Row 2: _ **N** _ _ **W** _ _ _
Row 3: _ **U** _ _ **O** _ _ **S**

PUZZLE #5: PHRASE FINDER

Find the words hidden in the word search that will help you to fill in the boxes and complete the common phrase. The words may be forward, backward, or diagonal.

a

```
F A R W T W Y H
W O O I E I E T
E R N H K B D R
G P T D N E H A
S A B S E N C E
M A K E S R G H
```

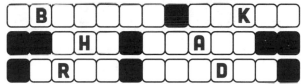

b

```
J Q E V S U P U
T H U R O F T E
T S I T T I N G
I T G A K H O D
Y N E K W U L E
O S B E Y O U R
```

PUZZLE #6: PHRASE FINDER

Find the words hidden in the word search that will help you to fill in the boxes and complete the common phrase. The words may be forward, backward, or diagonal.

a

```
F E H A E G U G
E L S M S O N N
U R I H Y I W U
E T Y E V A H F
R I E A S O E A
A B H R E R N H
```

```
■ □ □ M □ ■ □ L □ □ □ ■ ■
■ H □ □ □ ■ Y □ □ ■ A □ □ ■
■ □ □ V □ □ □ ■ □ U □ □ ■
```

b

"MARRIAGE" MIGHT HAVE A NICE RING TO IT, BUT...

```
K F O G T T G A
W U R S I N E K
Y O E I E R B E
S B P R E Q L V
D I A M O N D S
T I N G T S D T
```

```
■ □ □ □ □ M □ , □ □ □ ■ A □ □
A □ □ I □ □ □ □ □ S □ □
■ □ □ □ □ R □ □ □ □ ■ ■
```

PUZZLE #7: PHRASE FINDER

Find the words hidden in the word search that will help you to fill in the boxes and complete the common phrase. The words may be forward, backward, or diagonal.

a

```
V A F D E S Y E
F P L A Y I N G
E E N J H D H F
Y G N T H E H O
S O O C D S S M
D B W Y E R I H
```

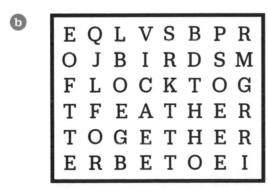

b

```
E Q L V S B P R
O J B I R D S M
F L O C K T O G
T F E A T H E R
T O G E T H E R
E R B E T O E I
```

WE ALL NEED SOMEBIRDY TO PREEEEN ON. ♫

PUZZLE #8: PHRASE FINDER

Find the words hidden in the word search that will help you to fill in the boxes and complete the common phrase. The words may be forward, backward, or diagonal.

ⓐ

```
S R H A T G U G
E E S O S H S W
D T W H N D A U
E T Y T A E H N
R E E E S R O A
T B H R E D E H
```

> WHEN BUYING CABBAGE TO MAKE COLESLAW FOR A PARTY...

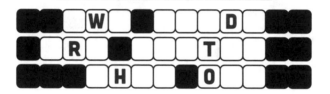

ⓑ

```
K H L V S B W P
O T A N D R V I
T C O V U E E G
E Y O O E K I G
I A Y K A N R T
E R T C Y O E O
```

PUZZLE #9: SCRAMBLES

Letters and words can be knots too! They can also be just as challenging to untie. Unscramble the letters to make words and/or proper names that relate to a common theme. Warning: Some words can be unscrambled to form multiple words, but only one relates to the theme!

a

ENLECADVL
`C L E V E L A N D`

LBIENR
`B E R L I N`

HAGOCENAR

COLNLNI

NLOOND

DMRAID

EPOIXHN

WGLOSGA

YSDEYN

UNHOOLLU

b

RUPMEI

DUREORGN

LTIREP

AESNSO

UGDOTU

TSRIEK

CPTERIH

ROUIFMN

GANERAM

EOLTFDIU

PUZZLE #10: SCRAMBLES

Unscramble the letters to make words and/or proper names that relate to a common theme. Warning: Some words can be unscrambled to form multiple words, but only one relates to the theme!

a

SREJOFNFE

NEEDYKN

RATUNM

DALFEGIR

ODNIMAS

TRARCE

LIONTCN

LEOTVERSO

HONNJSO

RIGHAND

b

LANIPEC

BOTSASALR

ERAPATKE

KOUOCC

STUHHR

GONEPI

RAMALDL

TORREOS

THUTHANC

CALFNO

PUZZLE #11: SCRAMBLES

Unscramble the letters to make words and/or proper names that relate to a common theme. Warning: Some words can be unscrambled to form multiple words, but only one relates to the theme!

a

ANSUED

AGOLET

SRUDCAT

FUTRELF

FOEFTE

KCEPUCA

IOCEOK

ACORNOMA

WINOBER

DULTSER

b

LERRICEN

SHECIA

OCCHU

MONTOTA

YEADDB

THCUH

OBOESACK

CHOKMAM

MAORREI

TREEDWAB

PUZZLE #12: SCRAMBLES

Unscramble the letters to make words and/or proper names that relate to a common theme. Warning: Some words can be unscrambled to form multiple words, but only one relates to the theme!

a

RHERYC

RUNTACR

NORGEA

NEPPEIPAL

ANNABA

HECLEY

VAAGU

TUQAKMU

SMENPIMOR

CROPATI

b

CLIMEYNK

SLEEHN

NOKKILED

REEVETS

TWENYHI

HENGONRER

MOSPULY

CLOBERAH

TWERSLIH

IVUSSEVU

PUZZLE #13: TRIVIA WORD FINDER

Word searches aren't all about straight lines and obscure vocabulary. Try mixing things up a bit and taking the path less traveled.

Find **SEVEN EIGHT-LETTER MOVIE TITLES** word-winding their way from the top row all the way down to the bottom row. The first answer is filled in to get you going.

....

....

....

....

....

....

S	G	G	T	F	S	P
U	O	R	A	W	R	U
P	D	E	I	N	E	P
Z	E	L	M	T	D	E
I	I	R	L	A	A	R
L	B	G	I	S	M	T
A	L	N	H	I	O	A
D	S	A	T	R	A	N

Find **SIX SIX-LETTER EUROPEAN CAPITALS** word-winding their way completely across the board from left to right. The first answer is filled in to get you going.

....

....

....

....

....

....

P	T	Y	E	N	S
A	I	H	D	I	N
L	A	S	R	O	D
M	C	D	B	S	T
W	Y	R	S	N	W
L	A	D	N	A	A
B	O	E	D	I	N
V	I	N	V	O	K

PUZZLE #14: TRIVIA WORD FINDER

Two major advantages to taking the path less traveled: 1) you get to feel like a bit of a rebel and 2) you might pioneer the "more-often-traveled path of the future."

Find **SEVEN SEVEN-LETTER MAMMALS** word-winding their way completely across the board from left to right. The first answer is filled in to get you going.

....

....

....

....

....

....

R	A	F	C	A	L	N
L	U	C	F	O	O	O
B	E	R	I	H	O	U
C	A	O	T	B	O	D
W	A	R	P	A	R	G
G	A	R	S	L	L	R
H	O	M	I	T	E	A

Find **SIX SEVEN-LETTER ADJECTIVES** word-winding their way from the top row all the way down to the bottom row. The first answer is filled in to get you going.

....

....

....

....

....

O	A	T	S	C	P
F	W	T	H	R	A
E	F	I	Y	U	R
B	S	L	R	D	E
E	I	O	S	F	E
A	S	M	T	N	U
T	E	H	T	Y	L

PUZZLE #15: TRIVIA WORD FINDER

Two major advantages to taking the path more often traveled: 1) it's probably more stable (which means no bushwhacking will be involved) and 2) you might meet up with a friend!

Find **SEVEN SEVEN-LETTER ELEMENTS** word-winding their way from the top row all the way down to the bottom row. The first answer is filled in to get you going.

··

··

··

··

··

··

··

H	T	N	P	T	F	C
I	Y	L	I	U	H	L
T	A	D	N	T	U	R
A	T	R	G	O	R	O
I	N	S	O	R	M	O
I	N	G	T	I	G	I
U	E	U	E	N	U	E
M	M	N	E	N	M	N

Find **SIX U.S. STATE CAPITALS** word-winding their way completely across the board from left to right. The first answer is filled in to get you going.

··

··

··

··

··

··

D	I	R	A	T	E
P	E	L	V	N	A
A	T	N	E	E	A
T	L	P	U	K	R
A	O	B	T	O	Y
S	O	S	A	N	N
B	N	W	I	L	G
L	A	S	L	N	O

PUZZLE #16: CHAIN GAME

Find a chain of linked words to make one complete clockwise path all the way around the letter grid so that you **ONLY USE ADJECTIVES** and **EVERY WORD STARTS WITH THE LAST LETTER OF THE PREVIOUS WORD.**

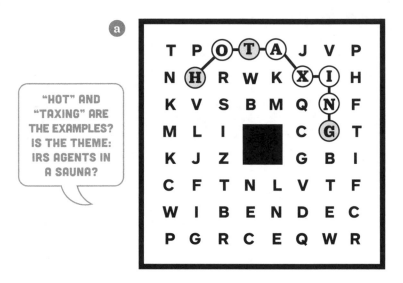

"HOT" AND "TAXING" ARE THE EXAMPLES? IS THE THEME: IRS AGENTS IN A SAUNA?

Find a chain of linked words to make one complete clockwise path all the way around the letter grid so that you **ONLY USE SIX–LETTER WORDS** and **EVERY WORD STARTS WITH THE LAST LETTER OF THE PREVIOUS WORD.**

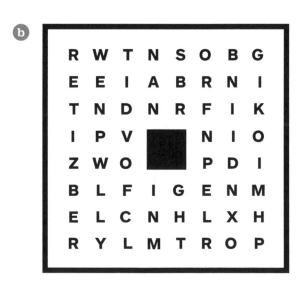

PUZZLE #17: CHAIN GAME

Find a chain of linked words to make one complete clockwise path all the way around the letter grid so that you **ONLY USE** FRUITS AND VEGETABLES and **EVERY WORD STARTS WITH THE LAST LETTER OF THE PREVIOUS WORD.**

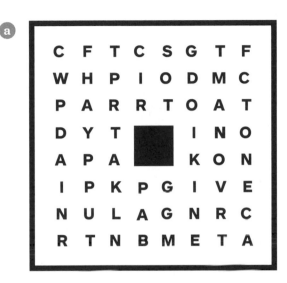

Find a chain of linked words to make one complete clockwise path all the way around the letter grid so that you **ONLY USE** ANIMALS and **EVERY WORD STARTS WITH THE LAST LETTER OF THE PREVIOUS WORD.**

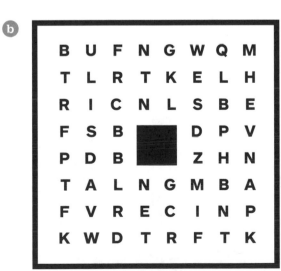

YOU'VE GOT ALL THE KOALAFICATIONS TO SNAIL THIS PUZZLE!

PUZZLE #18: CHAIN GAME

Find a chain of linked words to make one complete clockwise path all the way around the letter grid so that you **ONLY USE** HERBS AND SPICES and **EVERY WORD STARTS WITH THE LAST LETTER OF THE PREVIOUS WORD.**

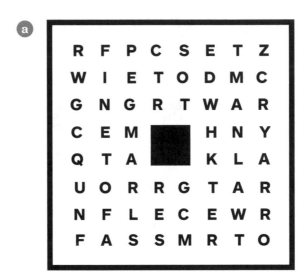

Find a chain of linked words to make one complete clockwise path all the way around the letter grid so that you **ONLY USE WORDS** WITH DOUBLE LETTERS and **EVERY WORD STARTS WITH THE LAST LETTER OF THE PREVIOUS WORD.**

FLEXIBILITY IS ESSENTIAL FOR THESE NEXT PUZZLES...

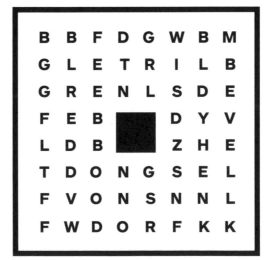

PUZZLE #19: CHAIN GAME

Find a chain of linked words to make one complete clockwise path all the way around the letter grid so that you **ONLY USE SPORTS TERMS AND EQUIPMENT** and **EVERY WORD STARTS WITH THE LAST LETTER OF THE PREVIOUS WORD.**

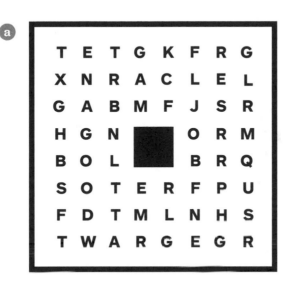

Find a chain of linked words to make one complete clockwise path all the way around the letter grid so that you **ONLY USE TWO-SYLLABLE WORDS** and **EVERY WORD STARTS WITH THE LAST LETTER OF THE PREVIOUS WORD.**

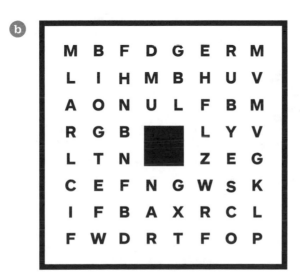

...THEY'RE LIKE "FOOTLOOSE" FOR YOUR PEN!

PUZZLE #20: COMPASS CROSSWORD

Complete the crosswords below by filling in the answers, one letter per square, in the direction stated in each clue.

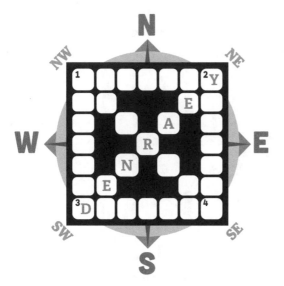

a

1 East
This wheel gets the grease

1 Southeast
Lawman

2 Southwest
Desired strongly

3 North
"A Christmas Carol" author

4 North
Lightning bug

4 West
Scandinavian country

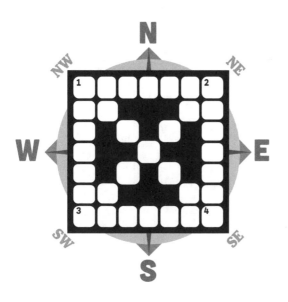

b

1 East
Able to be heard

2 South
Flows over and encloses

3 North
An exact reproduction

3 Northeast
Love affair

3 East
Takes away

4 Northwest
A grassland with scattered trees

PUZZLE #21: COMPASS CROSSWORD

Complete the crosswords below by filling in the answers, one letter per square, in the direction stated in each clue.

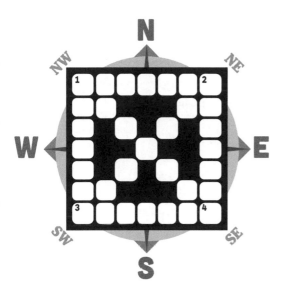

a

1 East
Battle boat

1 Southeast
Greet hospitably

2 South
Eau de toilette

2 Southwest
Little flute

3 North
Became too large for

3 East
Watch closely

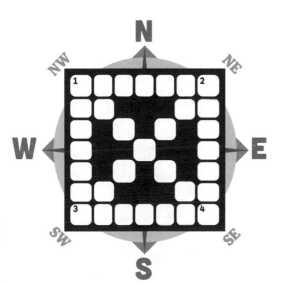

b

2 West
Noisy argument

2 Southwest
Foursome

2 South
Tonic water ingredient

3 North
Unrest

3 East
The way something feels

4 Northwest
Endless

PUZZLE #22: COMPASS CROSSWORD

Complete the crosswords below by filling in the answers, one letter per square, in the direction stated in each clue.

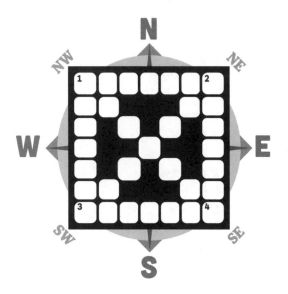

a

1 East
The study of animals

1 Southeast
Fervently partisan

3 North
Glamour, vitality

3 Northeast
Fowl

4 North
Unhealthily thin

4 West
.... comedy

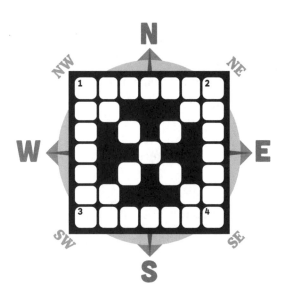

b

1 East
More humorous

1 Southeast
Mink coat maker

2 South
One who walks in the countryside

2 Southwest
Second draft

3 North
Aural warmer

4 West
Express great happiness

PUZZLE #23: COMPASS CROSSWORD

Complete the crosswords below by filling in the answers, one letter per square, in the direction stated in each clue.

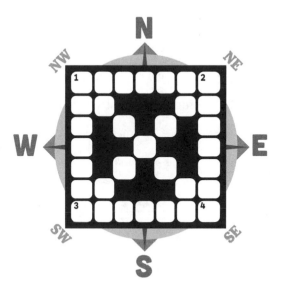

a

1 East
Not adhering to ethical principles

1 Southeast
Gave no attention to

2 Southwest
Menial worker

3 North
Stuffed pasta

4 North
Based on a system of ten

4 West
Unscrambler

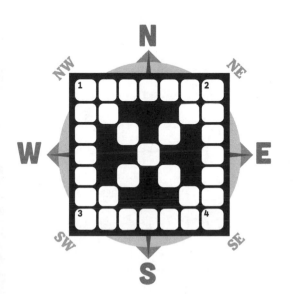

b

1 East
Powdered pimento seasoning

1 South
Sugar pill

2 South
Queasy on a plane

2 Southwest
Guacamole ingredient

3 East
Australian wilderness

4 Northwest
Tomato-based condiment

PUZZLE #24: LINKING WORDS

Just like stepping from stone to stone over a river, one slip here could land you in some trouble. Tread carefully during these next puzzles, using the clues and letters on the right to make word paths between like symbols that fill the board on the left.

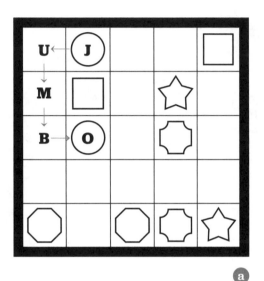

● Oversized

■ A covering of minute ice crystals

⬢ A small bag for carrying money

⬡ A confection made with sugar

★ Unpleasant sound

A	B	C	D	E
E	F	I	J	M
N	N	O	O	O
P	R	R	S	S
S	T	U	U	Y

ⓐ

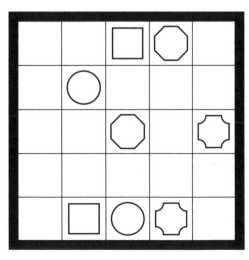

● Connection, link

■ A buyer and seller

⬢ An appearance that belies the truth

⬡ Exaggerated pride or self-confidence

A	A	A	B	C
C	D	E	E	E
F	H	H	I	M
N	N	R	R	S
S	T	U	U	X

ⓑ

PUZZLE #25: LINKING WORDS

Using the clues and letters below, make word paths between like symbols to fill the board.

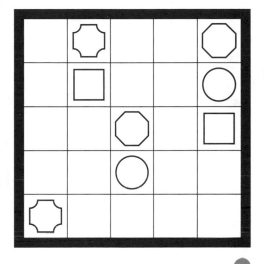

● Not easily bent

■ To release or detach oneself

⬢ A definite authoritative tenet

✚ The art or technique of making motion pictures

A A A C D
D D E E E
G G G G I
I I I M M
N N O R S

(a)

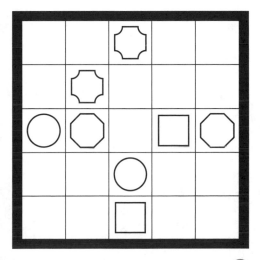

● A short trip taken to attend to some business

■ To make a short, harsh cry

⬢ A situation in which ending a disagreement is impossible

✚ To dress or groom oneself carefully

A A A C D
D D E E I
K K L M N
O P P Q R
R R S U W

(b)

PUZZLE #26: LINKING WORDS

Using the clues and letters below, make word paths between like symbols to fill the board.

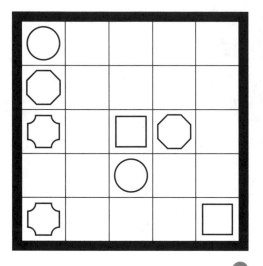

● One who is ardently attached to a cause, object, or pursuit

■ One given to greedy and voracious eating

⬣ To make a grant of money

⬣ Wet spongy ground

A B D E E
G G H I L
N N O O
O S S T T
T T U U W

ⓐ

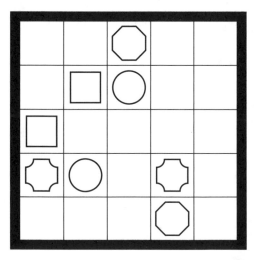

● A bird, or one who collects indiscriminately

■ A keen-edged cutting instrument

⬣ An unbound printed publication

⬣ To strengthen by heating and cooling

A A A E E
E E G H I
L M M M O
P P P P R
R R T T Z

ⓑ

PUZZLE #27: TRIVIA WORD SEARCH

Look closely and put on your trivia hat. For this next puzzle you'll need to find the answers to the clues on the bottom in the word search on top. Words may be found forward, backward, up, down, or diagonal.

```
M F N I N E T Y R H
C R A F C H E E R S
P A D C G J L N A H
M R L R E S T E I U
X A M C Y B L G D D
E N N R I I O W N S
L G H T N U Q O I O
O C P D L B M H K N
R U N I T E D S M C
```

1: This car company was founded in 1925.

2: This TV show, which made it to #1, was set in Boston.

3: This social networking site debuted in 2004.

4: This river flows past West Point Military Academy.

5: This watch company was founded in London, England, in 1905.

6: This is the fifth-most-abundant element in Earth's crust.

7: This New York Yankee was nicknamed "The Commerce Comet."

8: This U.S. airline is based in Chicago.

9: This is the square root of 8,100.

10: This is traditionally the longest river in the world.

11: This is the seventh-largest country in the world (1,269,346 square miles).

....

 **BRAIN FACT:** When you search for something in a visual scene, your brain can filter the incoming information so that anything that looks like the thing you are looking for "pops out" and draws your eyes to it.

71

PUZZLE #28: TRIVIA WORD SEARCH

Find the answers to the clues on the bottom in the word search on top. Words may be found forward, backward, up, down, or diagonal.

A LOCAL MAN ENTERED A PUN CONTEST. HE SENT IN TEN SEPARATE SUBMISSIONS...

A	N	A	C	O	N	D	A	D	U
T	A	B	A	C	U	S	T	R	G
C	O	E	M	K	Q	H	E	Y	N
N	G	R	S	E	Z	P	E	M	A
O	A	I	O	B	R	L	V	L	T
T	R	N	W	N	L	C	E	X	S
O	U	G	N	E	T	E	U	J	U
R	B	L	H	R	T	O	P	R	M
P	A	S	F	S	D	I	M	E	Y

1: This is the most populous city in Canada.

2: This English novelist wrote *Frankenstein*.

3: This island is located 27 miles north of Venezuela.

4: This sea separates Russia from Alaska.

5: This planet orbits the sun every 88 days.

6: This Ford first rolled off assembly lines in 1964.

7: This is a subatomic particle with a positive electric charge.

8: This counting device dates back centuries.

9: This is one of the largest snakes in the world.

10: This is an alloy of iron and carbon.

11: This South American country is divided into 25 regions.

12: This is what you call the U.S. coin with Roosevelt on it.

....

 **BRAIN FACT:** Your knowledge for facts and events, trivial or not, is called declarative memory. This type of memory is based on factual information (such as vocabulary) and your personal experiences.

PUZZLE #29: TRIVIA WORD SEARCH

Find the answers to the clues on the bottom in the word search on top. Words may be found forward, backward, up, down, or diagonal.

...IN THE HOPES JUST ONE WOULD WIN, BUT NO PUN IN TEN DID.

```
A R M T L L A M A M
C M W E F U S P A B
R O A N X T C D H P
U R D Z U I R A F A
G S J N O E C G S C
B E A X T N S O J I
Y E Q S C G H M D N
P B M G A L I L E O
P A R T O N V B L T
```

1: This *Star Wars* producer was born in Modesto, California, on May 14, 1944.

2: This sport has 7-, 13-, and 15-player-per-side versions.

3: This European city has 1,281 bridges.

4: This actor won an Academy Award for his role in *Scent of a Woman*.

5: This country-western singer and theme park owner was born on January 19, 1946.

6: This comic strip debuted on October 2, 1950.

7: This North American nation declared its independence on September 16, 1810.

8: This river discharges, on average, 7,381,000 cubic feet of water per second (more than any other river in the world).

9: This inventor developed the concept of the single-wire telegraph in the late 1830s.

10: This Italian, the "father of modern physics," was born on February 15, 1564.

11: This South American pack animal is related to the alpaca.

word skills
MASTER

CRITICAL THINKING

based in the frontal cortex

Any exercise that requires complex levels of planning, logic, sequencing, and/or reasoning

$$E = mc^2$$

what it does

Strengthens neural pathways in the brain that help you plan, take action, problem solve, and (hopefully) learn from and correct your mistakes

how it works

Critical thinking uses many different cognitive abilities, such as:

evaluation, interpretation

impulse control, social behavior

ANALYZING INFORMATION + **USING LOGIC** + **SYNTHESIZING INFORMATION** + **PROBLEM SOLVING** + **DEVELOPING STRATEGY**

appraisal, observation

inference, reasoning

explanation, decision making

PUZZLE #1: DOMINO THEORY

It's BrainCoach Oliver's turn to host game night for his friends, and he could use a little help setting up. While he breaks out the Stick Bombs™, can you place a full set of dominoes in the grid? Each "0" represents a blank, and each domino will appear exactly once in the finished grid. Use the chart to keep track of which dominoes you've already placed. Note: Three dominoes have been placed to get you started.

2	6	5	4	1	1	2	1
4	0	2	6	5	4	2	3
5	3	4	4	2	0	3	1
1	6	6	5	1	5	0	4
0	0	3	0	2	5	0	6
0	3	1	5	6	2	2	4
1	6	6	3	3	4	3	5

	0	1	2	3	4	5	6
6	√	√	√				
5							
4							
3							
2							
1							
0							

PUZZLE #2: CHILLIN' WITH MY GNOMIES

Cora has decided to paint her collection of garden gnomes. With her primer spray ready, and only enough paint to do one continuous line through the gnomes, she realizes that some of her special-edition gnomes have been mistakenly placed in the line of spray fire! Avoiding these special-edition gnomes, can you trace Cora's paint path (represented in the grid below) in less than two minutes? You may move up, down, and across, but never diagonally. You must pass through **EVERY** white square **ONLY ONCE**.

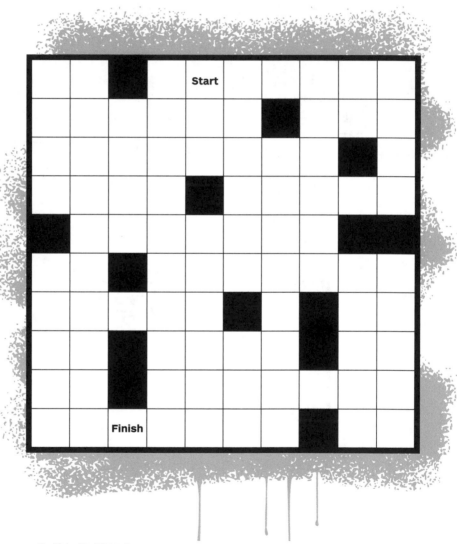

(Cheryl Graham/iStock/Thinkstock)

PUZZLE #3: WELL-READ

Follow the instructions below to reveal a quotation from the twentieth-century poet Wystan Hugh Auden.

EEL	LIVED	SOME	NOW
I	NOES	ABOVE	CATER
BOOKS	MIMIC	BRIEFLY	IRAQI
TRACE	CRATE	HEAL	ARE
EXPOSURE	SPRING	REVEL	UNFORTUNATE
GYM	UNDESERVEDLY	THY	MIX
DECAL	BEEF	VIVID	FORGOTTEN
MUSSEL	RHYTHM	HUMOROUS	WASTE
SANDWICH	ALOHA	NONE	NIGHT
STAGNATE	THROW	OREGANO	PERMANENT
VANE	BEFORE	REACT	ARE
BEAUTIFUL	ALE	EXTREME	PSST
INK	MILD	UNDESERVEDLY	DANTE
DASH	HART	MYTH	SCHOOL
NTH	REMEMBERED	TIMOTHY	STROP

1. Cross off all words that contain no vowels (A, E, I, O, U).

2. Cross off each word that can be rearranged to spell "CARET."

3. Cross off each word that becomes a new word when the letter "K" is placed in front.

4. Cross off each word that sounds the same as a part of the body.

5. Cross off each word that contains the name of an insect.

6. Cross off each word that is spelled using only Roman numerals.

7. Cross off each five-letter word that is also a word when read backward.

8. Cross off each word that begins and ends with the same vowel.

9. Cross off each word that can precede "BOARD" to form a common compound word or phrase.

10. Cross off each word that appears immediately above a three-letter word.

PUZZLE #4: CODE WORD

Code word puzzles are a lot like crossword puzzles, only instead of clues, you must crack a code in order to fill in each of the blanks. Each letter of the alphabet will have its own different numerical value; and all 26 letters will be used at least once to form common words and phrases in the chart below.

14	6	1 I	4	18	8	9	■	8	17	20	8	8
6	■	2 N	■	14	■	3	■	21	■	23	■	21
24	7	9	12	7	■	8	11	8	20	18	8	9
7	■	8	■	2 N	■	■	■	10	■	20	■	8
17	1 I	13	8	9	17	8	18	23	19	14	6	5
■	■	8	■	8	■	9	■	18	■	■	■	21
16	7	4	■	5	14	1 I	2 N	6	■	15	21	3
8	■	■	■	4	■	18	■	5	■	6	■	■
22	7	1 I	8	18	23	4	23	17	6	7	4	8
7	■	17	■	5	■	■	■	7	■	21	■	19
8	5	23	4	7	5	8	■	4	8	18	18	6
4	■	25	■	20	■	16	■	1 I	■	1 I	■	13
18	26	8	23	24	■	16	23	20	24	19	23	3

A B C D E F G H I J K L M N O P Q R S T U V W X Y Z

1 I	2 N	3	4	5	6	7	8	9	10	11	12	13
14	15	16	17	18	19	20	21	22	23	24	25	26

PUZZLE #5: CLOWNING AROUND

Five students at East Valley Clown College (Heather, Alice, Ben, Josh, and Mike) are very excited to start their next semester. When they compare their schedules, they discover that they will each be taking a different clowning class (Nose Honking 101, Lion Taming: Theory and Practice, Plate Spinning 205, The Art of Tumbling 104, and Fire Juggling 314) each day in the week. They also discover that no two students will be taking the same class on the same day, and that no two professors teach the same student on the same day. No two students ever have the same schedule! Using the grid below, can you complete the upcoming semester schedule?

	Betty	Cathy	Ellen	Jack	Chris
Monday			**BEN** FIRE JUGGLING		**HEATHER** LION TAMING
Tuesday		**MIKE** NOSE HONKING			
Wednesday	**BEN** PLATE SPINNING			**JOSH** LION TAMING	
Thursday		**JOSH** PLATE SPINNING			
Friday					**ALICE** PLATE SPINNING

(Jeremy/iStock/Thinkstock)

 **BRAIN FACT:** Research has shown that training in logical reasoning increases connectivity within your frontoparietal network, thus increasing your attention to context clues and goal-oriented stimuli.

PUZZLE #6: WORKING 9 TO 5

Take a break from your daily grind and fit these words and phrases into the grid. Two words are entered to get you started.

5 LETTERS

ACTOR	CRUMB	PIXIE	
ACUTE	DREAM	PIZZA	
ADIEU	ELITE	SHADY	
ADMIT	FLUTE	SOCKS	
ALIAS	HUMUS	SWAMI	
AMBER	HYENA	SWEEP	
AMONG	IMAGE	TABLE	
AMPLE	JEANS	TEASE	
AROMA	MAIZE	TETRA	
BASIC	PIECE		
CREPE	PIQUE		

9 LETTERS

BABY TEETH
EASTER EGG
MAINFRAME
MISTLETOE
NAME NAMES
SEED MONEY
SHAKE A LEG
SNOWFLAKE
SUPERNOVA

PUZZLE #7: WORD-DOKU

Solve this puzzle as you would any Sudoku puzzle—except this time with letters instead of numbers! Complete the grid so each row, column, and 3-by-3 grid contains the letters **ACDEINOTU**.

A					T			D
I			N	O				
T		D	E				C	O
			A				E	
E		T	D		N	A		U
	O				C	D		
C	A				E			
				D	A			I
N		U						E

As a bonus, what three nine-letter words can you spell with the letters **ACDEINOTU?**

 **BRAIN FACT:** There is a region in the occipito-temporal cortex called the visual word form area. This area is thought to process basic letter and word shapes, even though it evolved long before these symbols.

PUZZLE #8: BATTLESHIPS

In this game of battleships, blow your competition out of the water by locating the six ships listed below. To help you out, the numbers next to each row and column indicate the number of "hits" in that line of the chart, which includes ships already located. Each ship appears horizontally or vertically only, and no ships touch in any direction (including diagonally).

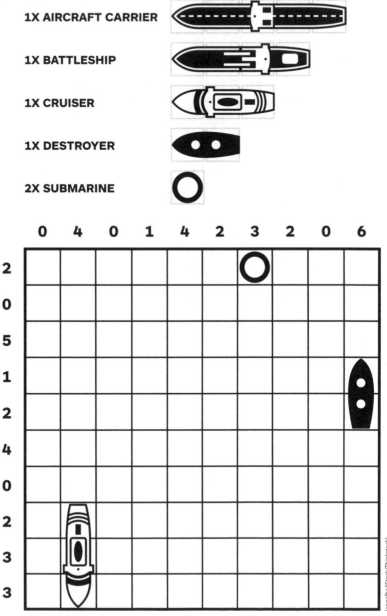

1X AIRCRAFT CARRIER

1X BATTLESHIP

1X CRUISER

1X DESTROYER

2X SUBMARINE

(angelha/iStock/Thinkstock)

PUZZLE #9: ROLL OF THE DICE

These aren't your average throwing dice. A different letter of the alphabet appears on each of the six sides of four dice. Each letter **appears only once**. Any side of a die can be face-up, and the dice can be in any order. Random throws produced the 15 words listed below.

BEND
BOXY
CAKY
FANG
FLAX
HOUR
JIVE
POET
PUCE
QUAD
RAIN
SNOW
THIS
VEAL
WORK

WHAT ARE THE SIX LETTERS ON EACH DIE?

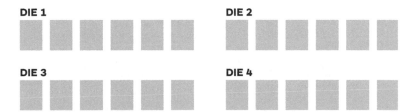

DIE 1

DIE 2

DIE 3

DIE 4

hint!

GET STARTED BY PLUGGING THE FOUR LETTERS OF ONE LISTED WORD INTO THE FIRST BLANK SPOT ON EACH OF THE FOUR DICE; THEN USE THE PROCESS OF ELIMINATION TO DISCOVER WHERE THE OTHER LETTERS GO.

PUZZLE #10: TWO-BY-TWO

These letters go marching two-by-two—hurrah! Form common four- and six-letter words by trading the two-letter pieces. Take all of the two-letter pieces from the six-letter words in A and add them to the two-letter pieces in B to form four-letter words. Then take all the pieces that are given in B and add them to the pieces in A to complete six-letter words. Do not change the order of the letters on the pieces. None of the answers will be proper names, contractions, or foreign words.

BONUS: Four two-letter pieces (two from A and two from B) will not be traded; when you've identified them, arrange the pieces (without changing the order of the letters on the pieces) to spell out an eight-letter phrase.

A. Six-letter words

UN		OL

		SH

AF		

	SA	ME

	OF	AH

	JE	CT

PI	GL	

BY		

B. Four-letter words

NO	

CO	RD

RU	

	TH

SE	

	ET

LO	

	OB

	RK

RA	

ID	

WO	

(Julie Weiss/iStock/Thinkstock)

BONUS: ....

🧠 **BRAIN FACT:** The right side of the brain is the creative side, right? Wrong. In truth, there are many types of creativity, and all depend upon networks that span the entire brain, not just one hemisphere.

PUZZLE #11: ALPHABETICAL ORDER

Think of this as a word search with an attitude and a penchant for wanderlust. Trace a continuous line from one black square to the other by passing through the letters of the alphabet in consecutive order **three times**, then find your way back by passing through the letters **in consecutive order** three more times. Diagonal steps and crossing of the two paths are permitted. Note: No square will be used more than once.

```
      J K L M N O P Q R H A B C D E F G H I J K Y
    O N M L K J I H G G O I C C V A B S T U V Y L M
  F G H Q D F C D M F D W C J J B R R Z U A X P Z Q O
  E E W C B B X Y E K G H K B B D Q R C V W Y X A Z P
  D V X A A Z C W U V R O L M A P B S F W A Z I B J Q
  U C Y Z ■ A B C S T T M U N O B T A W B X A G C F R
  V T B A Z Y X D E M F N X W V U M B V C B H D D E S
  W C S B C D E A B F K O P Q R S T M U D I L E G D T
  D X F R Q X V N G L G J K J F E D C I H F F M H C U
  E Y E R D P O E M P I H I M N L A J B A G W X Y B A
  F Z B C P F S M Q H A T J F O P K X Y Z H I J K L M
  G A A P A V E F C M B B C D E W V W E D D B A G N C
  M Z A B C D F G G L C S Z Y X B A U M J H O W O A R
  Y L M N O P Q H H K D T A Y D F B L T G H M P F N M
  Q X W V U T A I V J E U B Q Z H C T E S R Q W G L A
  P W O P Q R S J E I F V C R Z A P R A B C D X H K B
  O N A B C D E F G H G W X Y R I B C D E S E Y I J C
  M A B S T U V W X Y Z P J K E A B Z X F T K Z J I D
  L F C C D E F G H I J K L M N O P B Y X G H I E H E
  A K F G H J K L Q W V B H J W F E W Q W D J D E F F
  B D J E D C B A X A B U F G G A A D X C K C J Y G G
  C I L A F G H Y D C T D E H B C D E C L B Y Z N X H
  H B X Z C A Z E D S B C I J I H G F M B A ■ A B E W
  G F Y I B V B F R R A J K L T U V P N D Z A Z C F V
    E W C H C U Q Q Q K O N M L K J W O X B C B D U
      D E F G P O N M L A B C D E F G Y P Q R S T
```

BRAIN FACT: To solve the above puzzle, you'll be relying upon logic and your working memory (which is basically a short-term buffer to store a limited number of items temporarily).

PUZZLE #12: WATT'S THE DIFFERENCE

As part of her spring cleaning, Cynthia has decided to replace all the light bulbs in her apartment with more energy-efficient bulbs. In each of her **six rooms**, she listed every light fixture and made a note of the bulb's wattage. Even though each room had a different combination of bulbs (15, 25, 40, 60, or 75 watts), every room's bulbs **totaled 100 watts**.

Cynthia's bedroom fixtures do not take any bulbs of the same wattage as any in the bathroom, and the bathroom fixtures do not take any bulbs of the same wattage as any in the kitchen.

There are twice as many bulbs in the living room as there are in the guest room, and Cynthia's bedroom has twice as many as the bathroom.

The office has as many bulbs as the guest room and the kitchen combined.

How many bulbs, and of what wattage, are in each of Cynthia's six rooms?

PUZZLE #13: JIGSAW QUOTE

Answer the clues and transfer each letter to its corresponding box in the top grid. Some letters may appear in more than one answer word. Next, place the top diagram's eight squares into the bottom diagram in the proper order to reveal a quotation by Carlos Fuentes, a famous Mexican novelist.

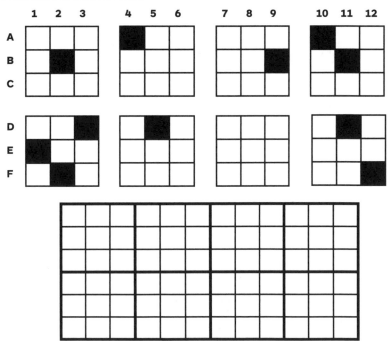

Guest Room

WATTS ....

Living Room

WATTS ....

Office

WATTS ....

Bathroom

WATTS ....

Cynthia's Bedroom

WATTS ....

Kitchen

WATTS ....

(Alisher Burhonov/iStock/Thinkstock)

1. Uncertain ___ ___ ___ ___ ___ ___ ___ ___ ___ ___
C9 A3 F10 E12 A7 E8 C12 B5 C10 F11

2. *Delta of Venus* author ___ ___ ___ ___ ___ ___ ___ ___
C7 B8 E7 D6 C6 B4 E11 A12

3. Smarty-pants ___ ___ ___ ___ ___ ___ ___ ___
E2 F8 E9 A1 A11 E12 A8 E4

4. Pecking order ___ ___ ___ ___ ___ ___ ___ ___ ___
B1 C12 D9 D1 E7 A3 B3 F7 D12

5. Done for ___ ___ ___ ___ ___ ___ ___ ___
B12 C2 D4 E10 B7 D10 C10 C8

6. Failure to communicate? ___ ___ ___ ___ ___ ___ ___ ___
F4 E3 B5 B10 A9 E6 A2 F1

7. State-of-the-art ___ ___ ___ ___ ___ ___ ___ ___
F3 E11 F1 F3 B6 F5 B3 C1

8. Minneapolis and St. Paul ___ ___ ___ ___ ___ ___ ___ ___ ___ ___
D7 B12 D6 C5 B3 F8 E6 C12 E4 F11

9. Recruiting specialist ___ ___ ___ ___ ___ ___ ___ ___ ___ ___
F3 D2 C2 D10 D8 C10 E5 B6 F10 C11

10. Trifling ___ ___ ___ ___ ___ ___ ___ ___ ___
C3 A6 F6 B8 A5 E7 F9 D7 C4

PUZZLE #14: FOUR-FIT

It takes a special kind of word to fit in a word puzzle: one that likes snug spaces and doesn't mind sharing some of their standing room. Fit these 40 four-letter words into the grid. One letter (X) is entered to get you started.

ACHE	FLIP	MALL	PEEL
AQUA	IAMB	MAMA	PICK
AXIS	JAMB	MANY	POUT
BIKE	JINX	MAYO	PUMP
BIRD	KIWI	MOJO	SOFA
DOES	KNIT	MUCH	THAW
EAVE	KNOB	NORM	TUBA
EBBS	LAZY	OBOE	UFOS
EDGY	LEAF	ONLY	WAXY
FINK	LOAF	OPUS	YOGA

PUZZLE #15: FLOOR TILES

Oh no! Game night is about to start, but Oliver dropped all of the dominoes on the kitchen floor! He counted them as he picked them up, and he's missing one—it must be under the fridge, out of reach.

Determine the arrangement of the dominoes in Oliver's tray, and identify the missing tile. Each "0" represents a blank. The chart will help you keep track.

4	6	4	5	2	5	1	4	4
1	2	2	1	6	6	3	5	0
3	3	0	0	3	2	3	0	6
6	1	2	6	0	1	1	5	6
1	4	3	4	3	4	2	4	5
2	0	5	3	2	0	0	1	5

	0	1	2	3	4	5	6
6							
5							
4							
3							
2							
1							
0							

ANSWER: ....

89

PUZZLE #16: CODE WORD

Spice up your daily crossword with a healthy dose of cryptography! Complete this crossword grid by cracking the simple code. Each letter of the alphabet has a different numerical value; all 26 letters are used to form common words and phrases.

8	5	14	17	23	2	5	3	20		25	23	22	15	1
5		23		10		21		25		5		10		26
11	18	22	1	3	10	6		11	18	17	26	18	12	20
11		20		20			22					5		3
6	18	11		10	20	18	3	6		24	13	14	22	18
		18				7				23		20		3
10	18	3	5	23		18	3	3		26	14	20	18	3
20			19	18	10		20	26	20					4
9	13	18	19	19		20	16	16		10	13	11	20	20
13		10		20			13					10		
5	14	17	13	10		3	5	12	5	22		23	10	16
1		15				7				13		19		4
5	25	5	22	18	22	20		18	5	10	4	5	14	20
22		21		14		20		11		16		22		20
20	4	20	12	6		16	23	22	22	23	25	1	13	11

A B C D E F G H I J K L M N O P Q R S T U V W X Y Z

1	2	3	4	5	6	7	8	9	10	11	12	13
14	15	16	17	18	19	20	21	22	23	24	25	26

PUZZLE #17: PATHFINDER

The most devious mazes don't need walls. There are five different symbols (▲ ■ ♠ ♥ ★) in the grid below. Trace a path from one gray square to the other gray square by passing through adjacent squares of the same design, then find your way back on adjacent squares of another design. Diagonal steps and crossing of the two paths are permitted.

♥	♥	★	■	♠	♥	♥	♥	♥	■	■	▲	▲	▲	♥
■	★	♠	★	♥	♠	♠	■	♠	♥	▲	♠	■	▲	■
■	♥	▲	♥	▲	♥	♠	★	♠	▲	♥	♠	♥	♥	■
★	■	♥	▲	▲	♠	♥	♥	▲	■	♠	♥	★	▲	■
▲	★		■	▲	▲	▲	▲	■	♠	▲	■	♥	■	■
★	▲	♠	♥	■	■	♠	■	★	■	▲	★	♥	★	♥
▲	★	♠	♥	♥	■	■	♥	♥	★	▲	♥	■	★	♥
★	♥	★	♠	♠	♠	♥	■	▲	♥	♥	▲	♥	♠	♥
★	▲	♥	★	★	■	♠	♥	★	▲	★	▲	★	♥	♠
★	▲	▲	♠	■	★	♠	▲	♥	♥	▲	♥	▲	★	♠
♠	★	▲	♥	■	★	♠	♠	▲	▲	♥	▲	★	♠	♥
♠	♠	▲	★	★	■	♠	■	■	♥	■	■	★	♠	♥
♠	▲	★	♥	■	♠	♠	★	★	♥	■	★	♠	■	♥
♠	★	♥	▲	■	♠	★	♠	♥	★	★	♠	♥	♠	■
▲	★	▲	♥	▲	★	▲	▲	♥	▲	♥	★	♥	■	♥
★	▲	★	★	★	■	♥	▲	♥	♥	★	♥	■	■	
★	■	♥	■	■	■	♥	♠	▲	▲	■	★	★	▲	★
★	★	■	■	★	★	■	■	♥	♥	▲	▲	▲	★	▲

. . . .

 **BRAIN FACT:** Critical thinking is a method of coming to a conclusion based on a reasoned process. It doesn't often look as neat as this puzzle, but it does often increase your gray matter (i.e., brain cells).

PUZZLE #18: BATTLESHIPS CROSSWORD

Your naval adventures continue! This puzzle combines two classics: battleships and crosswords! Complete the hidden crossword grid by answering the clues and using the coordinates to determine where the answers appear in the grid. A clue is a guaranteed hit; you will need to determine where the black squares are and which answers are across and which are down. (Note: Coordinates do not always designate the beginning of a word.)

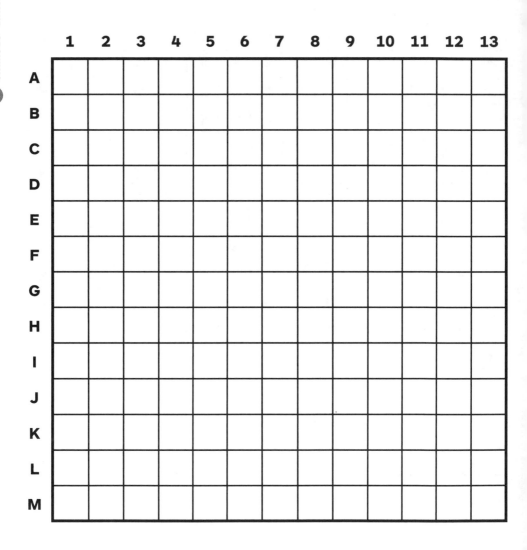

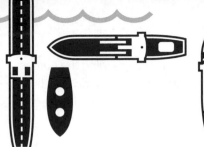

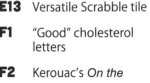

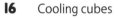

A4	Beaver's handiwork	**E13**	Versatile Scrabble tile	**I6**	Cooling cubes
A6	Shopping ctr.	**F1**	"Good" cholesterol letters	**I7**	Cooperative relationships
A8	Flow back	**F2**	Kerouac's *On the* ____	**I8**	"Catch my drift?"
A9	*Titanic*'s undoing	**F5**	Taxpayer ID	**I13**	Cement chunk
B3	He met a pieman	**F7**	Hit the slopes	**J1**	Engine part
B5	____ puppet	**F10**	NFL's Cardinals, on scoreboards	**J5**	Skunk giveaway
B9	Baseball stitching			**J7**	Dollar bill
B10	Lamb's cry	**F12**	Van Gogh's *Bedroom in* ____	**J10**	Abu ____
C4	Set of beliefs	**G5**	Not at all hard	**J12**	Folder projections
C7	Perfectly fine	**G6**	Big ____ Country	**K2**	Sleek horse
C12	Where leaf meets stem	**G9**	Big galoot	**K6**	Dopey
D1	Radar gun no.	**G11**	Bourgeois	**K9**	Wee drink
D3	Santa kisser of song	**H1**	*Doctor Who* network	**K11**	Overly confident
D5	Feeling sore	**H3**	Washbowl	**L4**	Take a bough
D9	Fail to keep up	**H8**	Maiden name preceder	**L5**	Midday
D13	Forest female	**H12**	WNBA position	**L8**	Dinghy pair
E3	Bear with a hard bed	**H13**	Slugger's stat	**M4**	Not post-
E6	Cunning	**I2**	Bowler feature	**M8**	Feathery wrap
E8	Longish blog post	**I4**	Dart thrower's asset	**M9**	Band aid?
E11	Tacks on			**M10**	Quick-witted

PUZZLE #19: CALCULATED WORDS

Every letter in the grid has a numerical value that can be calculated by adding the number of the row to the number of the column in which the letter appears. For example, a "T" is in the sixth row and the fourth column of the grid, and therefore has a value of 10. Other "T"s may have different values. Each 10 may stand for a different letter.

To discover the calculated words from Bertrand Russell (a British nobleman, philosopher, logician, mathematician, historian, social critic, and all-around overachiever), determine the proper letter for each number. Every letter in the grid will be used only one time.

	1	2	3	4	5	6	7
1	P	E	U	T	U	H	E
2	N	O	E	E	O	O	P
3	T	S	O	S	C	I	R
4	E	E	N	L	R	G	E
5	O	O	T	A	R	S	S
6	P	S	S	T	B	I	V

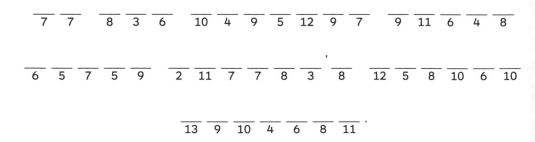

7 7   8 3 6   10 4 9 5 12 9 7   9 11 6 4 8

6 5 7 5 9   2 11 7 7 8 3 8   12 5 8 10 6 10

13 9 10 4 6 8 11 .

PUZZLE #20: SECRET IDENTITY

If spies had a favorite kind of word puzzle, this would be it. The answers to the clues and a bit of trivia have been hidden in a substitution code. Answer the clues and use the decoded letters to reveal other answer words and the trivia. The initial letters of the decoded words will spell out the answer to the trivia.

CLUES

CHOCOHOLIC'S SENSATION	OHSQF FHOK
STEREO ACCESSORY	KAQZWKTVAO
HIDDEN	THB TE OUSKB
MORTGAGE ARRANGEMENT	AOMFTY
LINK IN A CHAIN?	OBTFA
DERISIVE SOUND	KTTB
"DEFINITELY!"	UVZAAZ
WHERE SNOWBIRDS GO IN SPRING	VTFBK
VIEW OF TOLEDO PAINTER	AD SFAMT
COLLECTIBLE TOPPER	ITBBDA MQW
PERFECTLY	TV BKA VTOA
RED SEA REPUBLIC	JAGAV

TRIVIA

BKUO QDBAF AST TE MQFBTTV OHWAFKAFT HVZAFZTS ZAOBFTJO

BADAWKTVA ITTBKO YKAV KA MKQVSAO UVBT MTOBHGA.

ANSWER: ....

PUZZLE #21: DOUBLE TAKE

When you fill the correct missing letters into the crossword grid, those letters, transferred to the correspondingly numbered dashes below, will reveal a quotation by Jean Cocteau, a French poet. No word will be repeated in the grid, and all the words in the grid will be common English words: proper names, abbreviations, contractions, and foreign words do not appear. There are different possibilities to fill the grid, but only one way will give you the correct quotation.

Then again . . . the quotation may need a little reflection before it will make proper sense.

10	O	S	8	■	D	A	51	S	■	5	I	45	E	R
A	20	E	A	■	47	L	E	O	■	50	N	T	R	O
S	C	A	38	■	11	O	R	Y	■	S	T	O	21	35
17	A	46	A	N	G	41	E	■	24	L	O	12	D	E
■	■	22	E	E	D	■	B	E	E	■	Y	E	S	■
C	A	R	E	34	R	■	P	2	T	A	40	■	■	
4	L	E	■	D	E	36	E	R	■	39	A	W	N	1
S	L	9	W	■	26	A	27	E	16	■	P	A	13	L
43	Y	P	E	D	■	U	T	18	E	R	■	29	C	E
■	■	37	A	R	L	Y	■	D	25	N	T	E	D	
S	19	T	■	49	A	T	■	C	15	L	A	■	■	
33	R	E	A	7	Y	■	P	42	L	Y	G	30	O	32
E	48	A	S	E	■	H	6	D	E	■	3	A	V	E
N	O	44	E	S	■	O	P	E	N	■	E	V	23	N
T	R	E	31	T	■	14	E	S	28	■	D	A	R	T

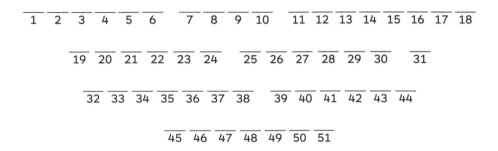

```
___ ___ ___ ___ ___ ___   ___ ___ ___ ___   ___ ___ ___ ___ ___ ___ ___ ___
 1   2   3   4   5   6     7   8   9   10    11  12  13  14  15  16  17  18

    ___ ___ ___ ___ ___ ___   ___ ___ ___ ___ ___ ___   ___
    19  20  21  22  23  24    25  26  27  28  29  30    31

    ___ ___ ___ ___ ___ ___ ___   ___ ___ ___ ___ ___ ___
    32  33  34  35  36  37  38    39  40  41  42  43  44

            ___ ___ ___ ___ ___ ___ ___
            45  46  47  48  49  50  51
```

PUZZLE #22: WORD-DOKU

Sudoku, incidentally, is just as fun with letters. Solve this puzzle as you would any Sudoku; so that each row, column, and 3-by-3 grid contains the letters **DEIMNSTUX**.

T					I			U
	I	M						
U			D	X	E			
	X			I		U		
I				D				N
		S		E			M	
			M	T	S			D
						E	S	
S				E				T

As a bonus, what two-word, nine-letter phrase can you spell with the letters
DEIMNSTUX?

 **BRAIN FACT:** Games like Sudoku can improve both your critical thinking and memory. Multiple studies with dementia patients have confirmed that these puzzles are more effective than drugs or supplements.

PUZZLE #23: BATTLESHIPS CROSSWORD

We return to the sea once more, mates! In this game of battleships, complete the hidden crossword grid by answering the clues and using the coordinates to determine where the answers appear in the grid. A clue is a guaranteed hit; you will need to determine where the black squares are and which answers are across and which are down. (Note: Coordinates do not always designate the beginning of a word.)

This crossword has a trivia element: Nine of the clues are a year (or years) that has some significance to that answer. What do these nine answers have in common?

	1	2	3	4	5	6	7	8	9	10	11	12	13	14	15
A															
B															
C															
D															
E															
F															
G															
H															
I															
J															
K															
L															
M															
N															
O															

ANSWER: ....

A2 Mosque bigwig

A4 1976

A7 Give a seat to

A10 Raison d'__

A13 Email status

B1 Office alert

B7 Snoozed

B9 Troy, NY, campus

B10 Vague abbr.

B13 Bottled water brand

B15 Affirm as true

C1 "__ little teapot…"

C3 Org.

C8 Schoolbook

C11 1968

C14 Cry in a kid's game

D2 Desert plateau

D4 Draw

D12 Last Supper cup

E5 Like an attentive dog's ears

E11 Look like a creep?

E14 1996

E15 Choreographer Tharp

F1 Run of luck

F2 Prefix with byte

F6 Loud slap

F9 Hawker's pitch

F12 Related to the lower back

G1 Catch sight of

G3 Piano piece?

G5 Not made up

G7 Circus clapper

G10 Mah-jongg unit

G15 "Close, __ no cigar"

H2 Face-to-face exam

H8 1988

H10 Movie music

H13 Greasy spoon fare

H15 *The Cosby Show* son

I1 Highlands hat

I3 1928

I6 Drawn tight

I9 Separately

I14 Short and snappy

J5 Expertise

J6 Mix, as a drink

J12 Shoelaces alternative

J14 WWII ally

K2 Weeper of Greek myth

K4 1920

K7 Resell to desperate fans, say

K10 Feel intuitively

K12 1952

L1 Plumb tuckered out

L5 Iron-rich meat

L8 Diamond spoiler

L1 Camper's shelter

L12 Productive

L14 College on the Thames

M3 1932, 1984

M5 *Show Boat* composer Jerome

M7 Lamb's mama

M10 Song section

M15 Jotted message

N2 "Yeah, right!"

N3 Soap box?

N6 Generation __

N8 Up and about

N13 Necktie feature

N15 UFO pilots, presumably

O1 Butterfly snares

O4 Gym duds

O6 Sunday seats

O9 Tries to find

O13 1992

O14 Fleming and McKellen

(angelha/iStock/Thinkstock)

PUZZLE #24: WELL-READ

Follow the instructions to reveal a quotation from William Safire, an American author.

SHOGUN	IF	MICE	BEGAN
I'VE	TIGER	STATUETTE	FIXATE
DOUGH	BILLIONAIRE	MADCAP	TOLD
YOU	GLOVE	PLATES	OWE
WAKEN	GEESE	ONCE	TERRIER
TROT	WHOA	SIZE	I'VE
TOLD	YARN	SCOWL	GOOSE
HAMPER	YOU	LEAPFROG	SIMOLEONS
TRAPEZE	PONY	A	MOWED
STAPLE	PASTEL	FIRE	FEET
THOUSAND	CUPFUL	BEAU	TIMES
STEPFATHER	RESIST	PADRE	CAMPFIRE
FOOT	MOUSE	UNANNOUNCED	PALEST
BORON	GIGGLING	HYPERBOLE	BATHER
VISIBILITY	HOLE	TOE	VACATE

1. Cross off each two-syllable five-letter word that becomes a one-syllable word when its center letter is removed.

2. Cross off each six-letter word that can be divided into two new three-letter words.

3. Cross off each word that contains the name of an animal.

4. Cross off each word that rhymes with "SHOW."

5. Cross off each word that becomes a new word when an "E" is inserted between its first and second letters.

6. Cross off each word that contains the letters "PF" together.

7. Cross off each word that is an anagram of the word "PETALS."

8. Cross off both the plural and singular of each word that appears in the diagram in both forms.

9. Cross off each word that can follow "FOX" to form a common compound word or phrase.

10. Cross off each word that contains four of the same letter.

PUZZLE #25: PYRAMID SCHEME

While this pyramid likely won't last for centuries once it's finished, it will definitely be easier for you to build on your own. Each brick in the pyramid should contain a value equal to the sum of the two bricks directly below it. Can you fill in the empty bricks?

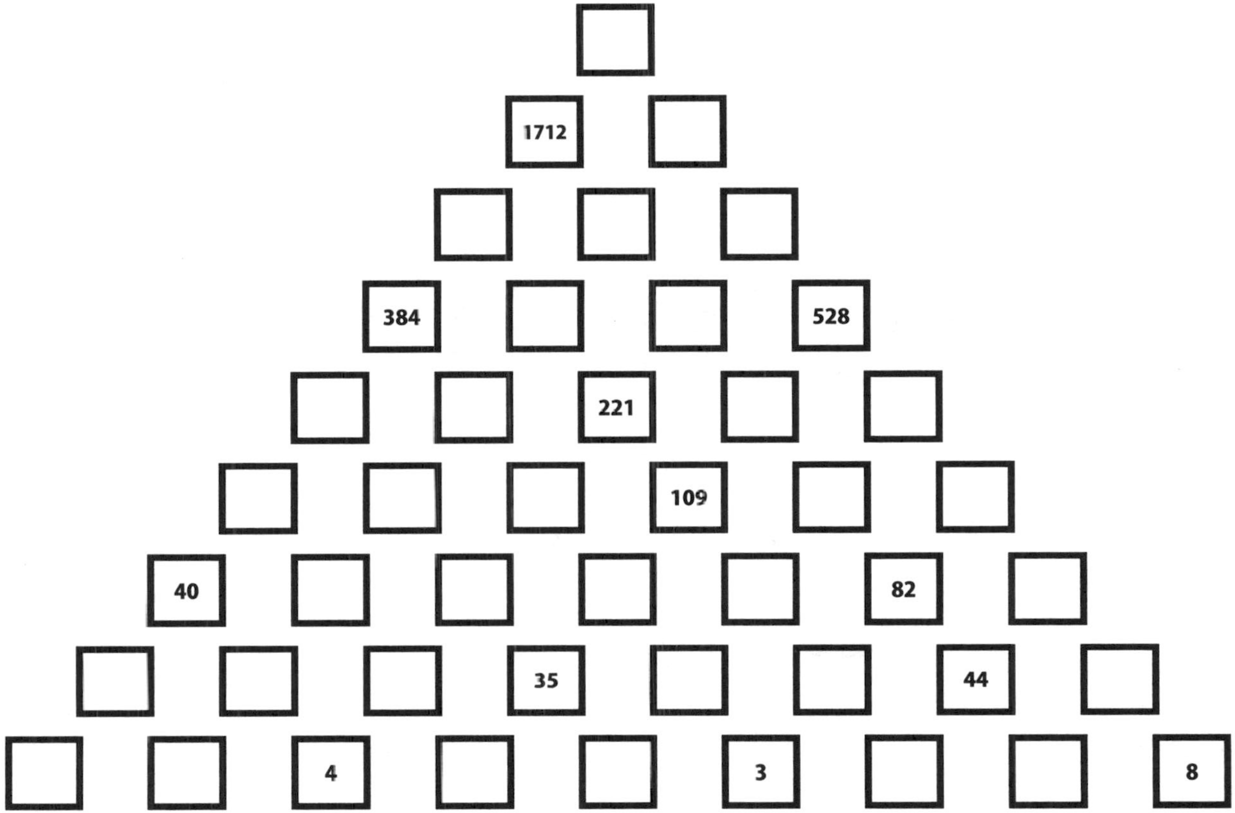

8

44

82

3

528

109

221

35

1712

384

4

40

PUZZLE #26: ROLL OF THE DICE

Laws of Probability imply that if these dice were rolled enough, they would spell out Shakespeare's complete works.

A different letter of the alphabet appears on each of the six sides of four dice. Each letter appears only once. Any side of a die can be face-up, and the dice can be in any order. Random throws of the dice produced the 12 words listed below.

BEAD
FURL
JOSH
MYTH
NAVY
NEXT
POCK
QUIP
SLAB
VOID
WINK
WORD

WHAT ARE THE SIX LETTERS ON EACH DIE?

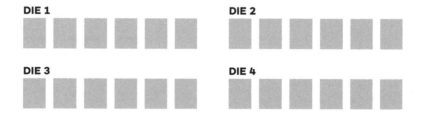

DIE 1

DIE 2

DIE 3

DIE 4

....

 **BRAIN FACT:** Does all this statistical thinking leave you feeling uncomfortable or mentally drained? Great! That means you are strengthening your neural connections—and maybe even creating new ones!

PUZZLE #27: CALCULATED WORDS

Every letter in the diagram has a numerical value that can be calculated by adding the number of the row to the number of the column in which the letter appears. For example, an "R" is in the fourth row and the seventh column of the diagram, and therefore has a value of 11. Other "R"s may have different values. Each 11 may stand for a different letter.

To discover the calculated words from Samuel Taylor Coleridge, an English poet and literary critic, determine the proper letter for each number. Every letter in the diagram will be used only one time.

	1	2	3	4	5	6	7	8
1	P	S	E	O	D	S	D	B
2	B	R	S	E	R	O	Y	R
3	O	E	T	E	H	H	S	O
4	R	O	D	I	D	O	R	T
5	E	T	S	T	R	E	S	S
6	I	E	W	B	T	R	H	R
7	T	N	T	S	E	W	I	I
8	R	E	N	I	R	E	P	I

___ ___ ___ ___ ___   ___ ___   ___ ___ ___ ___ ___   ___ ___
15 5   4   7   8   16 3   13 8   4   7   10   15 9

___ ___ ___ ___ ___   ___ ___ ___ ___   ___ ___ ___ ___ ___ ;
6   9   10 14 7   9   12 12 7   6   12 9   6   10

___ ___ ___ ___ ___ ___   ___ ___   ___ ___ ___   ___ ___ ___ ___
2   11 6   8   13 9   12 13   10 8   4   3   11 5   9

___ ___ ___ ___ ___   ___ ___   ___ ___ ___ ___ ___   ___ ___ ___ ___
9   5   11 8   11   8   11   11 13 5   7   10   10 14 8   12

___ ___ ___ ___ ___ .
10 14 6   7   9

PUZZLE #28: PLANE DEALING

This past year has been a busy (and expensive!) one for the six pilots who rent hangars at Wallace Field. Each of their planes (Mooney M20J, Piper Archer, Cessna Skyhawk, Beech Baron, Cirrus SR22, and Aeronca Champ) needed major repairs as part of its annual service (resealing of leaky fuel tanks, complete engine overhaul, replacement of landing gear motors, radio upgrade, replacement of vacuum pump, and autopilot upgrade) plus a new paint job (white, red with white stripes, green with blue stripes, yellow, blue with a red tail, green with black wings).

From the information given below, can you determine the pilot who rents each hangar (1001, 1002, 1003, 1004, 1005, and 1006), his or her type of plane, the major repair the plane needed, and the plane's new color scheme?

1. The autopilot needed to be upgraded for the plane in the hangar farther west than both Chuck's hangar and the hangar that houses the Cirrus SR22.

2. Of the three hangars on one side of the runway, one is the hangar where the fuel tanks needed to be resealed, one is 1003, and one houses the Beech Baron.

3. The radio upgrade was performed in a hangar on the same side of the runway as, and immediately between, Chris's hangar and the hangar with the yellow plane.

4. The Cessna Skyhawk is directly across from the plane that needed the engine overhaul. The Mooney is blue with a red tail.

5. One pilot south of the runway owns the green plane with black wings and another pilot owns the Champ; neither pilot is Lane, who lives on the south side.

6. Hangar 1005 is northeast of both Paul's hangar and the hangar where the plane needed new landing gear motors.

7. Nellie's hangar is between the pilot who had to replace the vacuum pump and the pilot who owns the plane that is red with white stripes.

8. Harriet's hangar is across the runway, but not directly across, from the hanger where the Piper Archer is housed and is east of, and on the same side of the runway as, the plane that needed a radio upgrade.

9. Of the six hangars, Lane's is in a corner diagonally opposite that of the one that houses the white plane.

10. Of the six pilots, the one who owns the green-and-blue plane rents a hangar in a corner diagonally opposite that of the pilot who owns a yellow plane. The green-and-blue plane and the plane that needed the engine overhaul are on the same side of the runway.

1001

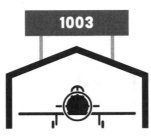

PILOT ....
PLANE ....
REPAIR ....
COLOR ....

1003

PILOT ....
PLANE ....
REPAIR ....
COLOR ....

1005

PILOT ....
PLANE ....
REPAIR ....
COLOR ....

1002

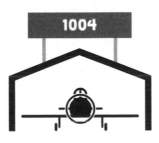

PILOT ....
PLANE ....
REPAIR ....
COLOR ....

1004

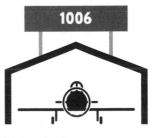

PILOT ....
PLANE ....
REPAIR ....
COLOR ....

1006

PILOT ....
PLANE ....
REPAIR ....
COLOR ....

(panic_attack/iStock/Thinkstock)

COORDINATION

the brain-body connection formed in the cerebellum

---

what it is

Balance, rhythm, spatial orientation, and the ability to react to auditory and visual stimuli have all been identified as elements of coordination.

woo-hoo!!

---

what it does

You use coordination for everyday tasks like brushing your teeth or driving a car—anytime your muscles work together to create movement.

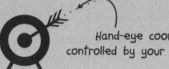

Hand-eye coordination is controlled by your fine motor skills.

Large muscle movements are coordinated by your gross motor skills.

---

how it works

Exercise increases the production of neurochemicals in your system, stimulating and strengthening your brain and increasing your reasoning and judgment.

 + =

(exercise) + (neurochemicals) = (new growth) + (better judgment)

PUZZLE #1: DOMINANT-EYE TEST

Like your hands, you also have a preference for which eye to use. This might be surprising because it appears that both eyes are hard at work together, but in fact, one is always playing more attention than the other. For most activities, there is no significant advantage or disadvantage to having a dominant eye, but for certain sports (like archery, shooting, golf, darts, and/or any activity that involves your accuracy and dexterity), knowing which eye is dominant may actually "up" your game.

To find your dominant eye:
Make a diamond shape with both of your hands. Next, with both eyes open, focus on an object through the center of the diamond. Close one eye, and then the other. You'll notice that when you close one eye, your nondominant eye will lose focus, but your dominant eye will still view the object clearly.

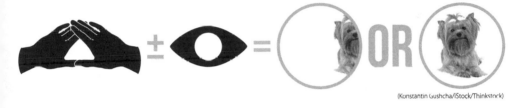

(Konstantin Gushcha/iStock/Thinkstock)

PUZZLE #2: PARALYZED-FINGER TRICK 1

Bend your middle finger under and lay the rest of your hand as flat as possible on a hard surface. Then, one at a time, try lifting your thumb, index finger, and pinkie. No problem, right? Now try lifting your ring finger. If it seems impossible, don't worry; it is.

See, all the tendons in your fingers are independent from one another, except for the tendons in your middle and ring fingers. While these tendons start as two separate parts of your body, they merge into one somewhere in the middle of the back of your hand. Thus, when your middle finger is folded under, your tendon is already flexed, and you cannot flex it again by lifting your ring finger.

PUZZLE #3: BEST LAME JOKE EVER

Remember math class back in third grade? Oh-so-careful plotting of the horizontal x-values and the vertical y-values to make something known as a "coordinate system," something which was very important because somehow it was going to help you later in life. Well, it's later in life. For this next puzzle, use the grid below to plot and draw lines between coordinate pairs in order to create a rather punny answer. If everything goes according to plan, it won't take you long to discover what may henceforth be referred to as the "best lame joke ever." Note: The first one is done for you.

① From (-10, 6) to (-8, 6) and (-10, -5) to (-8, -5)
② From (-9, 6) to (-9, -5)
③ From (3, 4) to (5, 6) to (6, 6) to (8, 4) to (8, -3) to (6, -5) to (5, -5) to (3, -3) to (3, 4)
④ From (0, 4) to (-2, 6) to (-3, 6) to (-5, 4) to (-5, 1) to (0, 0) to (0, -3) to (-2, -5) to (-4, -5) to (-5,-3)

⑤ From (-13, 1) to (-12, 3) to (-12, 4) to (-13, 6) to (-16, 6) to (-16, -5) to (-13, -5) to (-11, -3) to (-11, -1) to (-13, 1) to (-16, 1)
⑥ From (11, -5) to (11, 6) to (16, -5) to (16, 6)

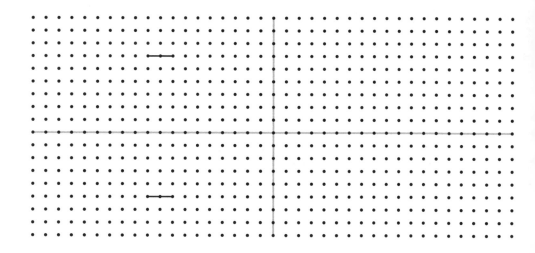

QUESTION: WHAT DID THE BUFFALO SAY TO HIS SON
WHEN HE DROPPED HIM OFF AT SCHOOL?

 ANSWER: ☐ ☐ - ☐ ☐ ☐

BRAIN FACT: Visually guided movements are processed in the aIPS region in the back of your brain. It works with your motor cortex and spinal cord to move your body toward visual targets.

PUZZLE #4: MEMORY FLIP-BOOK

In the Memory section of this book, you're going to be working to strengthen your focus and attention, but right now those pages will be used to boost your hand-eye coordination! In this next puzzle, let your eyes control, guide, and direct your hands through the Memory section to find the letters that will spell, in order, a word related to this combination of your skills.

In Memory Puzzle #3, what is the second letter of the first state listed?

A or **E**

In Memory Puzzle #21, what is the first letter of the title?

M or **R**

In Memory Puzzle #2, what is the third-to-last indicated letter?

K or **L**

In Memory Puzzle #17, which letter is equal to the number 24?

A or **I**

In the first Memory Puzzle #20, what is the first letter in the last logo shown?

G or **W**

In Memory Puzzle #13, what is the fourth letter in the last magazine title on the page?

A or **O**

In Memory Puzzle #5 continued, what is the fourth letter of the fifth question?

L or **M**

ANSWER:

🧠 **BRAIN FACT:** Memory-guided movements are processed in a different brain circuit than visually guided movements, but they still rely on your stored visual information for motor planning and control.

PUZZLE #5: BODY LANGUAGE

Normally things like facial expressions and posture—i.e., body language—mean you don't have to literally spell things out for someone to get your meaning; but for this next puzzle, that's not the case. In fact, you will have to use your whole body to very literally spell out the answer. So get good and limbered up, because this puzzle is going to require some flexibility, a floor-length mirror, and a bit of imagination.

1 Stand straight, feet together, facing the mirror. Hold your left arm out in front of you so it's perpendicular to your shoulder. Keeping your elbow next to your side, bend your right arm so it forms a 90-degree angle with your shoulder. Turn to your right side. Record this letter.

2 Stand straight, feet together, facing the mirror. Hold your left arm flush with your left side. Hold your right arm out at your right side so it's perpendicular to your shoulder. Try to bend your right arm into the top half of a semicircle shape. Record this letter.

3 Sit down with your legs straight in front of you, feet together, facing left. Hold your left arm out in front of you so it's perpendicular to your shoulder. Keeping your elbow next to your side, bend your right arm so it forms a 90-degree angle with your shoulder. Record this letter.

4 Stand straight, feet together, facing the mirror. Pretend you're holding a beach ball with your arms above your head. Drop your right arm down, without losing the semicircle shape, until it rests at just above your hips. Record the letter formed only by your arms.

5 Stand straight, facing the mirror. Raise both arms straight above your head, almost as if they are a straight continuation up from your legs. Record this letter.

ANSWER: ▶ ■ ■ ■ ■ ■

PUZZLE #6: A SHOW OF HANDS

American Sign Language (ASL) is a visual means of communication for many Americans. You've probably seen it around, maybe even studied it back in grade school, but would you be able to identify any of the alphabet letters all by yourself? For this next puzzle, find out as you follow the directions to spell out an answer that will relate back to those dexterous hands of yours. (And feel free to do some outside research if necessary.)

1. Hold your right hand so your palm is facing you. Fold your pinkie into your palm and cover it with your thumb. Make sure the three fingers remaining upright are slightly splayed. Record this letter.

2. Make a loose fist with your right hand, but be sure to tuck your thumb directly underneath the bottoms of your four fingers so that your thumbnail and pinkie touch. Record this letter in the second and ninth answer boxes.

3. Hold your right hand so your palm is facing you. Fold down your pinkie, ring finger, and middle finger. Make sure your index finger and thumb form a 90-degree angle. Record this letter twice.

4. Hold your right hand so your palm is facing you. Fold down your pinkie and ring finger. Fold over your thumb so it touches your middle finger at its first knuckle. Turn your hand to the left and let your wrist go limp. Make sure that your middle finger points down and your index finger points right. Record this letter.

5. Hold your right hand so your palm is facing you. Fold down your pinkie, ring finger, and middle finger. Make sure your index finger and thumb form a 90-degree angle. Record this letter.

6. Make a fist with your right hand, but be sure to place your thumb upright on the rightmost side of your index finger. Record this letter.

7. Hold your right hand so your palm is facing you. Fold down your ring, middle, and index fingers. Record this letter.

8. Hold your right hand so your palm is facing you. Using your pinkie, ring finger, middle finger and thumb, create a spherical shape in the center of your palm. Record this letter.

ANSWER: ▢ ▢ ▢ ▢ ▢ ▢ ▢ ▢

111

PUZZLE #7: THERE ISN'T ANOTHER LIKE IT

Welcome to the grid. Well, not that grid. For starters, there's significantly less neon here. Use the grid below to plot and draw straight lines between coordinate pairs (as directed in the following steps), then use your work to help answer the question that follows.

① From (-14, 14) to (-6, 14)
② From (-14, 1) to (-6, 1)
③ From (-17, -2) to (-12, -2)
④ From (-8, -2) to (-2, -2)
⑤ From (0, -2) to (6, -2)
⑥ From (10, -2) to (16, -2)
⑦ From (-17, -15) to (-11, -15)

⑧ From (5, -15) to (11, -15)
⑨ From (5, 12) to (6, 14) to (9, 15) to (12, 15) to (14, 12) to (14, 9) to (11, 4) to (5, 0) to (-1, 4) to (-4, 9) to (-4, 12) to (-2, 15) to (1, 15) to (4, 14) to (5, 12)

⑩ From (-10, 14) to (-10, 1)
⑪ From (-5, -15) to (-5, -2)
⑫ From (-14, -2) to (-14, -15)
⑬ From (-12, -2) to (-5, -15)
⑭ From (3, -2) to (8, -9)
⑮ From (8, -9) to (8, -15) and (13, -2)

WHO DESIGNED THIS FAMOUS LOGO?

ANSWER:

PUZZLE #8: PARALYZED-FINGER TRICK 2

Another way to demonstrate the "paralyzed-finger" phenomena:
Place the palms of your hands together and line up your fingers so they are parallel to one another. Next, fold down your middle fingers so the knuckles touch. Then, one at a time, "tap-tap" the finger pads of your thumbs, index fingers, and pinkies. Now, try doing the same with your ring finger. (Still impossible, right?)

PUZZLE #9: TAKE A DEEP BREATH

Remember the page at the beginning of this book with just the words "(deep breath)"? You thought it was just a joke, but did you know that deep breathing may actually keep your mind from wandering and improve your concentration? For this next puzzle, there's no trick or catch; the only answer you'll find is how to destress your brain "muscles."

1. Find a comfortable, quiet place (or create one by closing your eyes) and sit down. (Note: If you're going to close your eyes, do not do this while driving or operating heavy machinery.)

2. Try to relax and steady your breath.

3. Focus on one thing as fully as possible. (Tip: If your overloaded schedule, your attention-seeking kids, or the instant Internet gratification train stops you from focusing on just one thing, try slowly counting to yourself.)

4. Keep breathing slowly and evenly as deep as you can. Try to get as much air in your lungs as possible. Continue to focus and breathe for another 5 to 10 minutes.

5. Repeat as you like, because each time you do, your body will experience a full oxygen exchange that can help lower your heartbeat and stabilize your blood pressure—not to mention relax your mind.

PUZZLE #10: FROM POINT A TO POINT B

In geometry, the fastest way from point A to point B is a straight line; but in life, it's not always that easy. For this next puzzle, navigate a finger through the maze from point A to point B as fast as you can. (Note: If this seems too easy for your brainy self, don't worry; it's supposed to be.)

BEST TIME: ....

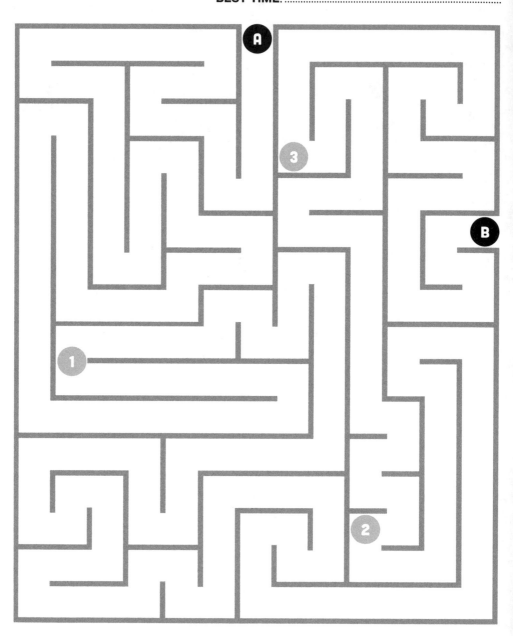

PUZZLE #11: VISUAL PERCEPTION FLIP-BOOK

You probably already had an eye-opening experience in the Visual Perception section of this book, but now it's time to use those pages to boost your hand-eye coordination as well! For this next puzzle, let your eyes control, guide, and direct your hands through the Visual Perception section to discover the letters that will spell, in order, a word that relates to some prominent parts of any face.

a In Puzzle #5, what is the first letter in the name of the second example picture?

B or **F**

b In Puzzle #1, what is the third-to-last letter in the first answer?

e or **n**

c In Puzzle #15, what is the first letter of the last person's last name?

a or **r**

d In Puzzle #24, what is the third-to-last letter shown as part of the rebus?

E or **T**

e In Puzzle #13, what is the fifth letter in the name of the first image?

m or **u**

f In Puzzle #2, what is the seventh letter of the first state photo shown?

N or **R**

g In Puzzle #23, what is the second-to-last letter in the last name of the last answer?

E or **I**

h In Puzzle #8, what is the first letter in the answer to the eighth image?

h or **s**

ANSWER: ▢ ▢ ▢ ▢ ▢ ▢

PUZZLE #10: FROM POINT A TO POINT B continued

Wait a second, didn't you just do this maze a few pages ago? For this next puzzle, go back to page 114 and complete the same maze again, only this time, test your spatial understanding by **ONLY LOOKING AT THIS PAGE AS YOU NAVIGATE**. Feel free to check yourself at points 1, 2, and 3. Did you end up where you thought you would?

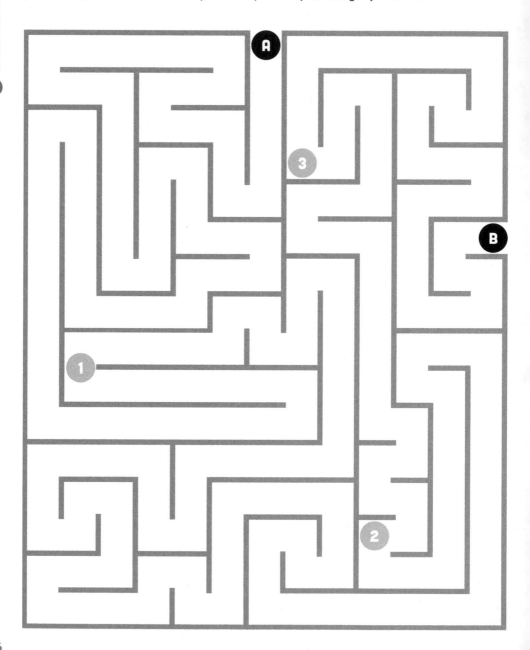

PUZZLE #12: A SHOW OF HANDS

Get ready to bust out your ASL skills again! For this next puzzle, follow the directions to spell out an answer that will (once more) relate back to those nifty hands of yours.

(1) **Using your right hand, point to the left using both your index finger and your middle finger. Record this letter.**

(2) **Make a loose fist with your right hand, but be sure to place your thumb upright on the rightmost side of your index finger. Record this letter.**

(3) **Hold your right hand so your palm is facing you. Fold down your pinkie and ring finger. Fold your thumb atop your ring finger. Fold your middle and index fingers down atop your thumb. Record this letter.**

(4) **Hold your right hand so your palm is facing you. Using your pinkie, ring finger, middle finger, and thumb, create a spherical shape in your palm. Record this letter.**

(5) **Hold your right hand so your palm is facing you. Fold down your ring, middle, and index fingers. Record this letter.**

(6) **Hold your right hand so your palm is facing you. Fold down your pinkie, ring, and middle fingers. Place your thumb on the rightmost side of your middle finger. Fold your index finger down atop your thumb. Record this letter.**

(7) **Hold your right hand so your palm is facing you. Fold down your pinkie and ring fingers. Cross your index and middle fingers, index over middle. Record this letter.**

(8) **Hold your right hand so your palm is facing you. Fold down your ring, middle, and index fingers. Place your thumb across your middle and index fingers. Record this letter.**

(9) **Using your left hand, create a semicircle shape. Be sure to keep your fingers together, but separate from your thumb. Record this letter.**

(10) **Make a peace sign with your right hand so that your palm is facing you. Move your thumb in between your middle and index fingers. Record this letter.**

ANSWER: ▢ ▢ ▢ ▢ ▢ ▢ ▢ ▢

PUZZLE #13: 625 DOTS-TO-DOTS

The aim of the game is to sequentially connect the dots and create a picture—and if that seems too easy for you, try using your nondominant hand for even more of a coordination workout!

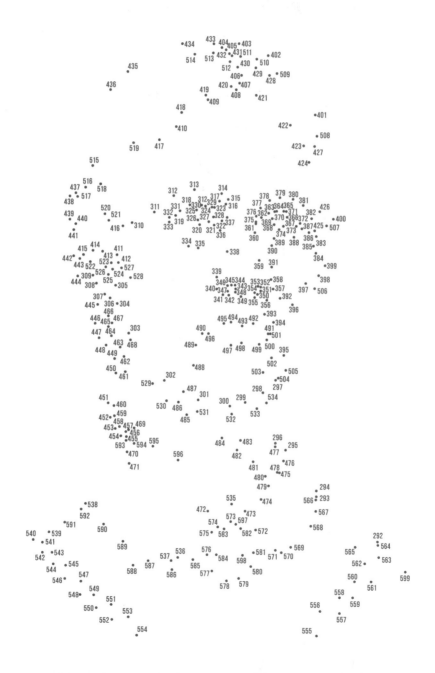

253 252
201 202 251
200 203 204
250
254 199 205 249
198 206
255 197

211 210
184 183 182 212 242 209 248 12 13
188 244 11 21 22 14
185 187 189 190 181 35 243 34 33 245 30 19 20 10
50 49 256 186 43 42 191 241 225 224 223 222 247 31 23
51 62 61 48 196 162 163 172 164 165 213 36 235 236 234 240 221 32 246 207 29
52 63 60 74 257 171 179 173 174 166 39 38 226 237 239 238 231 8 9 208 24
53 64 71 47 170 178 177 175 176 167 180 83 85 37 227 228 229 230 220 7 131 28 25
70 59 46 169 168 192 82 86 1 214 218 219 27
72 75 76 160 193 81 102 87 2 215 216 217 6 130 26 15
69 58 77 195 3 5 18 17
68 67 159 194 103 88 4 132 150 16 151
65 57 78 79 80 100 101 125 129 133
66 99 89 124 128 127 149
54 55 56 104 96 95 94 93 92 91 90 112 126 152
98 97 122 123 113
258 105 117 116 121 115 114 111 134
158 118 120 110 135 148
106 107 119 108 109 137 136 138 141 143 147 280
139 140 142 144 145 146
157 279 267
288 287 156 153 281 268
289 259 155 154 266 278 269
286 285 283 282 265
260 284
615 261 270
614 616 262 263 264 271
617 618
290 272
291 601 273 274
602 605
604 606 275
607 619 625
603 620 624
608 621 623 622
610
600 609
611
612 613 277 276

PUZZLE #14: CRITICAL THINKING FLIP-BOOK

You already built your logic and reasoning skills in the Critical Thinking section, but now it's time to use those pages to boost your hand-eye coordination as well! For this next puzzle, let your eyes control, guide, and direct your hands through the Critical Thinking section to discover the letters that will spell, in order, a word related to your brilliant mind.

1. **In Critical Thinking Puzzle #11, what is the ninth letter in the title?**

F	OR	I

2. **In Critical Thinking Puzzle #20, what is the eighth letter in the trivia answer?**

E	OR	N

3. **In Critical Thinking Puzzle #17, what is the third letter in the title?**

L	OR	T

4. **In Critical Thinking Puzzle #5, what is the fifth letter in the name of the class that Mike studies on Monday?**

E	OR	O

5. **In Critical Thinking Puzzle #3, which consonant appears the most in the title of the puzzle?**

W	OR	L

6. **In Critical Thinking Puzzle #13, what is the fourth letter in the name of the author of the quote?**

L	OR	O

7. **In Critical Thinking Puzzle #22, reading across from left to right, what is the sixth letter in the third line of the grid?**

E	OR	I

8. **In Critical Thinking Puzzle #8, what is the first letter of the thing you are trying to blow out of the water?**

C	OR	S

9. **In Critical Thinking Puzzle #28, what is the last letter in the name of the person who flies the Cessna Skyhawk?**

S	OR	T

ANSWER: ☐ ☐ ☐ ☐ ☐ ☐ ☐ ☐ ☐

PUZZLE #15: BODY LANGUAGE

Time to bust out that flexibility, floor-length mirror, and imagination again, as once more, you will be using your whole body to very literally spell out an answer to yourself. Hint: This answer is going to be a rather physical one.

1 Stand straight, feet together, facing the mirror. Hold your left arm out in front of you so it's perpendicular to your shoulder. Keeping your elbow next to your side, bend your right arm so it forms a 90-degree angle with your shoulder. Turn to your right side. Record this letter.

2 Stand straight, feet together, facing the mirror. Hold your left arm flush with your left side, and your right arm flush with your right side. Record this letter.

3 Stand straight, feet together, facing the mirror. Hold your left arm out at your left side so it's perpendicular to your shoulder. Hold your right arm out at your right side so it's perpendicular to your shoulder. Record this letter.

4 Sit down with your legs and knees together, directly beneath your bottom. Lean forward onto the palms of your hands. Try to hold your torso at a 45-degree diagonal angle between your shoulders and knees. Lift your legs up so they are parallel to your arms. Record this letter.

5 Sit down with your legs straight in front of you, feet together, facing left. Hold your left arm out in front of you so it's perpendicular to your shoulder. Keeping your elbow next to your side, bend your right arm so it forms a 90-degree angle with your shoulder. Record this letter.

6 Stand straight, feet together, facing the mirror. Pretend you're holding a beach ball with your arms above your head. Drop down your right arm, without losing the semicircle shape, until it rests just above your hips. Record this letter two times.

ANSWER:

121

PUZZLE #16: THINK OUTSIDE THE BOX

For this puzzle, follow the directions below to create your own paper alphabet block, then unscramble the letters to spell an adjective relating to intelligence.

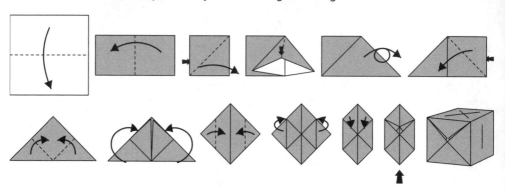

INSTRUCTIONS NOTE: THE GRAY SIDE REPRESENTS THE PATTERNED SIDE; THE WHITE SIDE, THE PUZZLE ON THE REVERSE OF THIS PAGE.

ANSWER: ▷ ▢ ▢ ▢ ▢ ▢ ▢

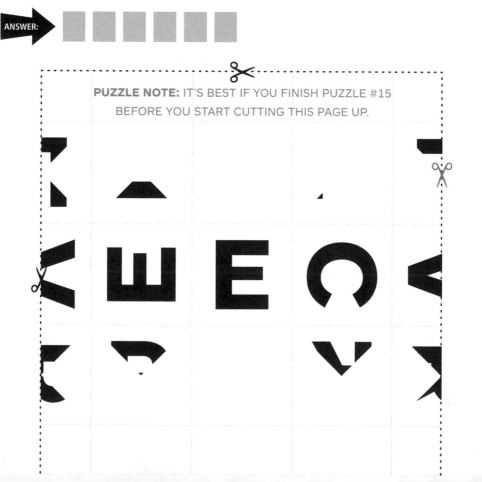

PUZZLE NOTE: IT'S BEST IF YOU FINISH PUZZLE #15 BEFORE YOU START CUTTING THIS PAGE UP.

PUZZLE #17: FROM POINT A...

PUZZLE #17: ...TO POINT B continued

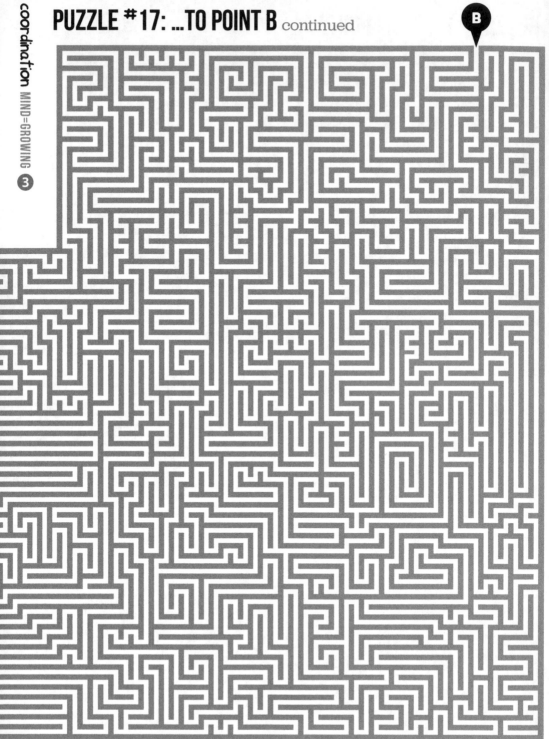

PUZZLE #18: A BRITISH SHOW OF HANDS

Many people think sign language is a worldwide universal language, but that's far from the case. In actuality, sign language can be just as regional as any spoken language. The British version, for example, is called finger spelling and has a two-handed alphabet.

For this next puzzle, it is advisable that you brush up on your British finger-spelling skills, because without them you will be rubbish, and with them you will spell out the answer.

1. Orient both your hands palms out and fingers together. Fold down your pinkie and ring fingers, then tuck under your thumbs. Place the two fingers remaining up on your right hand over the two fingers remaining up on your left hand at a 90-degree angle. Record this letter in the first answer box.

2. Hold your left hand palm up at a 45-degree angle. Hold your right hand so you're pointing with only your index finger. Using the tip of the index finger on your right hand, pull the tip of the middle finger on your left hand toward the right. Record this letter in the second, fifth, and tenth answer boxes.

3. Hold your left hand palm up at 45-degree angle. Make a loose fist with your right hand, being sure to face your fingers away from you, as well as tuck your thumb under. Using the pinkie on your right hand, pull the pinkie on your left hand (just above the knuckle) toward the right. Record this letter in the third, fourth, and twelfth answer boxes.

4. Hold your left hand palm up at a 45-degree angle. Hold your right hand so you're pointing with only your index finger. Using the tip of the index finger on your right hand, pull the tip of the ring finger on your left hand toward the right. Record this letter in the sixth answer box.

5. Hold your left hand palm up at a 45-degree angle. Hold your right hand so you're pointing with both your index finger and your middle finger. Place the two fingers on your right hand in the palm of your left hand. Make certain the two fingers on your right hand are parallel. Record this letter in the seventh answer box.

6. Make a loose fist with your right hand. Using your thumb and index finger, create a semicircle shape. Record this letter in the eighth answer box.

7. Hold your left hand palm up and your right hand palm down. Place your right palm on top of your left palm at a 90-degree angle. Then slide your right hand off the fingertips of your left hand. Record this letter in the ninth answer box.

8. Hold your left hand so you're pointing with only your index finger. Hold your right hand in a loose fist. Using the thumb and index finger on your right hand, create a circular shape. Place the tip of your left-hand index finger beside the tip of your right-hand thumb. Record this letter in the eleventh answer box.

WHEN VISITING ENGLAND, WHAT DO NUCLEAR SCIENTIST PENGUINS EAT?

PUZZLE #19: FLIPPING THE BIRD

According to Japanese tradition, if a person folds 1,000 paper cranes, their wish will be granted. Fortunately for you, you only need to fold one paper crane for this puzzle; but be sure to do it right, because you will need it to answer the question: "When the crane is facing left, what color is it?"

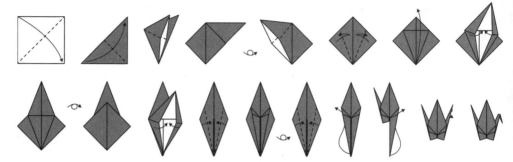

INSTRUCTIONS NOTE: THE GRAY SIDE REPRESENTS THE PATTERNED SIDE; THE WHITE SIDE, THE PUZZLE ON THE REVERSE OF THIS PAGE.

ANSWER:

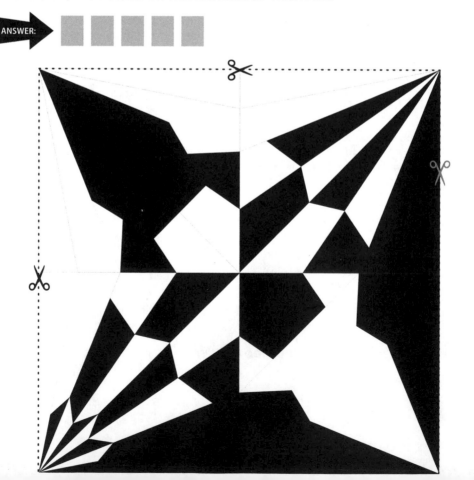

PUZZLE #20: BODY LANGUAGE

Time to bust out that flexibility, floor-length mirror, and imagination again; as once more, you will be using your whole body to very literally spell out an answer to yourself. Hint: This answer might be better answered by a cat forensic pathologist.

1 Stand facing left, feet together. Hold your arms out in front of you as if you are holding a beach ball parallel to your body (i.e., right curved arm over left curved arm). Drop your left arm down slightly, then raise your right arm up slightly. Ignoring your legs, bottom, and head, record this letter.

2 Stand straight, feet together, facing the mirror. Pretend you're holding a beach ball with your arms above your head. Relax your arms a bit so your hands are about six inches apart, then point your fingers upward. Ignoring your legs, bottom, torso, and head, record this letter in the second and sixth answer boxes.

3 Stand facing right, feet together. Using your left arm, create a semicircle between your shoulder and the top of your forehead. Make sure your left elbow is in front of your face. Hold your right arm out, pointing down at a 45-degree angle from your hips. Record this letter.

4 Stand straight, feet together, facing the mirror. Hold your left arm flush with your left side, and your right arm flush with your right side. Record this letter.

5 Stand straight, feet together, facing the mirror. Pretend you're holding a beach ball with your arms above your head and fingertips touching. Ignoring your legs, bottom, torso, and head, record this letter.

6 Stand straight, feet together, facing the mirror. Pretend you're holding a beach ball with your arms above your head. Drop down your right arm, without losing the semicircle shape, until it rests just above your hips. Record the letter formed only by your arms.

ANSWER:

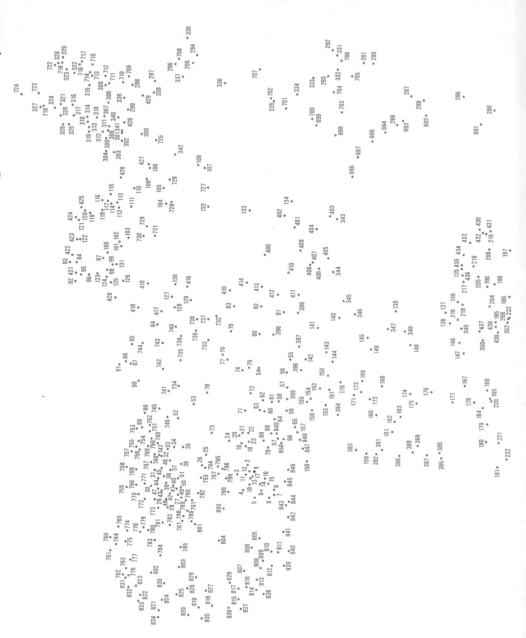

PUZZLE #21: 850 DOTS-TO-DOTS

Sequentially connect the dots to create a famous "Blue" painting—and if that seems too easy for you, try using your nondominant hand for even more of a coordination workout!

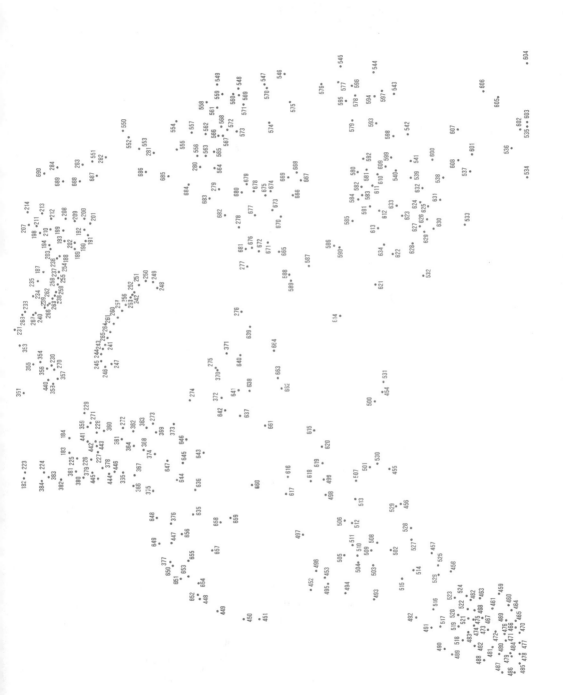

129

PUZZLE #22: WANDERING HANDS 1

Clench your fists together with your fingers interlaced. Lift up both your index fingers so they are **NOT** touching but are parallel to one another, then relax. (If you keep this up long enough, you'll notice your two index fingers slowly moving closer together!)

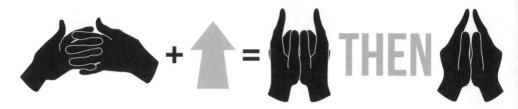

PUZZLE #23: WANDERING HANDS 2

Using the middle and index fingers on your nondominant hand, find the pulse at your wrist. Follow this pulse up to about the midpoint of your forearm, halfway between your wrist and elbow. (Feel free to mark this spot with something like a pen for the most accurate results.) With your dominant hand open but relaxed, as well as facing the ceiling, push down on the spot you located with the thumb of your other hand. Try several times with varying degrees of pressure. (If you keep this up long enough, you'll notice your relaxed hand will start to close—and maybe even "jump" up toward your wrist!)

BRAIN FACT: Alien hand syndrome is a rare neurological disorder where a person can have full sensation of their hand, but will report the hand as "belonging to, or being controlled by, someone else." A similar disorder, anarchic hand syndrome, occurs when people acknowledge ownership of the hand but still report instances where it seems to be moving of its own accord.

PUZZLE #24: MULTITASKING MADNESS 1

Move your right leg in counterclockwise circles and simultaneously draw the number 8 with your right hand. As you become more comfortable, try going faster. (If you keep this up long enough, you'll notice that your right foot will start to make clockwise circles!)

PUZZLE #25: MULTITASKING MADNESS 2

While sitting in a chair, lift your right foot off the floor and make clockwise circles. Once this is comfortable, begin to draw the number 6 with your right hand. (If you keep this up long enough, you'll notice that your right foot will start to move counterclockwise!)

PUZZLE #26: MULTITASKING MADNESS 3

Simultaneously rotate the index fingers of both your hands clockwise. Do it slowly at first, but then pick up speed. Move faster and faster! (If you keep this up long enough, you'll notice one finger will stop turning and start moving only up and down—or worse, start turning in the opposite direction!)

PUZZLE #27: THINK OUTSIDE THE BOX

Did you know that alphabet blocks are great for developing toddlers because they encourage hand-eye coordination, creativity, and spatial perception? Just because you're not a toddler anymore doesn't mean that alphabet blocks can't do the same thing for you—but there needs to be a twist! Like in the previous alphabet block puzzle, follow the directions below to create your own paper alphabet block, then unscramble the letters to spell one word related to both a unit of volume and the human body.

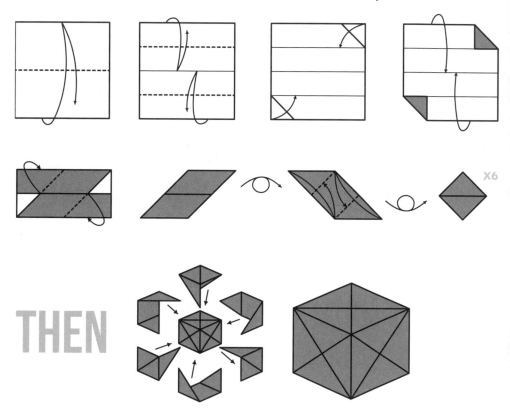

INSTRUCTIONS NOTE #1: THE GRAY SIDE REPRESENTS THE PATTERNED SIDE; THE WHITE SIDE REPRESENTS THE PUZZLE ON THE REVERSE OF THIS PAGE.

INSTRUCTIONS NOTE #2: WHEN FIRST FOLDING THE PATTERNED SQUARES, BE SURE TO FOLD THE PANELS WITH THE ALPHABET PIECES IN TOWARD THE CENTERLINE. THAT WAY YOU'LL HAVE FOUR LETTER "PIECES" FACING OUTWARD ON EACH SIDE WHEN YOU'RE DONE FOLDING.

ANSWER:

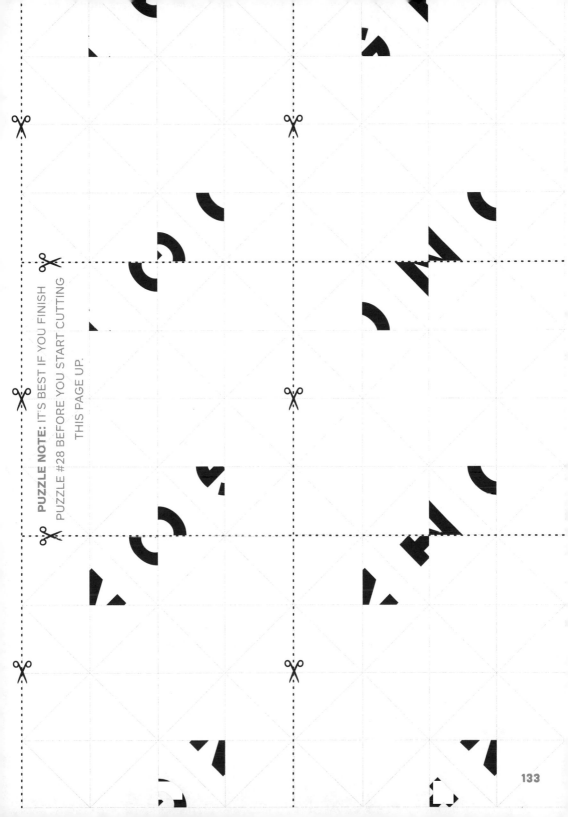

PUZZLE NOTE: IT'S BEST IF YOU FINISH PUZZLE #28 BEFORE YOU START CUTTING THIS PAGE UP.

PUZZLE #28: WORD SKILLS FLIP-BOOK

You're already a world-class word wrangler from the Word Skills section of this book, but now it's time to use those pages to boost your hand-eye coordination as well! For this next puzzle, let your eyes control, guide, and direct your hands through the Word Skills section to discover the letters that will spell, in order, a word related to gibberish.

1 **In Word Skills Puzzle #1, what is the third letter in the second word in the last paragraph of instructions?**

2 **In Word Skills Puzzle #15, what is the vowel that appears the most in the second puzzle grid shown?**

3 **In Word Skills Puzzle #4, what is the last letter of the first line of the last common phrase?**

4 **In Word Skills Puzzle #21, what is the middle letter of the answer to the North clue in the first puzzle shown?**

5 **In Word Skills Puzzle #12, what is the ninth-to-last letter in the instructions?**

6 **In Word Skills Puzzle #18, counting up from right to left, top to bottom, what is the twenty-sixth letter in the first letter grid?**

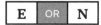

ANSWER:

PUZZLE #29: 440 DOTS-TO-DOTS

Sequentially connect the dots to spell out a message—and if that seems too easy for you, try using your nondominant hand for even more of a coordination workout!

coordination MASTER

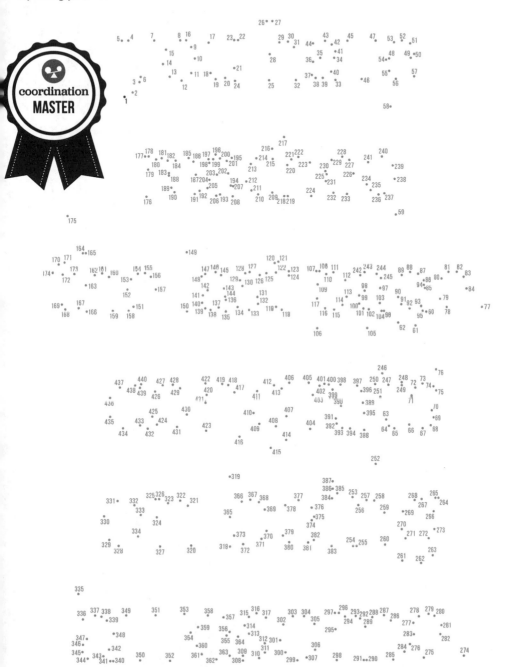

MEMORY

a brainwide process that's constructed in the temporal lobe

what it is

As a critical part of our sense of consciousness, memory exists as a process which begins with encoding, proceeds to storage, and ends in retrieval.

 → →

short-term memory
1. Very temporary (only lasts 2–30 seconds)
2. Part of working memory

working memory
1. Basis of intellect
2. Allows for sorting and manipulating of information

long-term memory
1. Lasts a few days to a few decades
2. Increased by placing importance on info

what it does

Improves your ability to learn information, and with mnemonic devices, can even improve your focus and attention rate

how it works

Data comes from different parts of your brain and is reassembled as a coherent whole.

"light bulb" + **BZZZZ** + 💡 + ☀ = 💡
(name)   (sound)   (shape)   (function)

PUZZLE #1: PLACEMENT IS KEY

Isn't it funny how you can use something every day but if asked to remember a specific detail, you may still struggle with it?

For this puzzle, try to determine which keys on a standard QWERTY keyboard are being talked about in the clues below. Feel free to peek at a keyboard if you need hints, but for the best brain workout, try using just your memory first. Determine the keys correctly and they will spell out the polite way to interrupt a keyboard.

FOLLOW THESE DIRECTIONS IN ORDER:

1. Record the key directly to the right of **X**.

2. Record the key up two rows and slightly to the left of **B**. Also record this in the seventh answer box.

3. Record the key below the numbers **4** and **5**.

4. Record the key one row below **P** and slightly to the left. Record this in the fourth, sixth, and tenth answer boxes.

5. Record the letter three keys directly to the left of **F**.

6. Record the letter one key directly to the left of **F**.

7. Record the letter two rows up and slightly to the right of **X**.

ANSWER:

....

🧠 **BRAIN FACT:** Your brain has multiple types of memory. For typing at lightning speeds on a keyboard, you use both your proprioceptive (sense of where your body parts are located in space) and motor memory.

PUZZLE #2: Y2K-ISH

Time is relative, they say. How quickly you can forget what you had for lunch on Monday or the password that required both a number AND a capital letter. *i4Get?* Listed below are various familiar objects or events. Determine which happened **BEFORE** the year 2000 AD and then use those letters in order to spell a message about the year 2000.

FOR EXAMPLE:
The Great Pyramid of Giza was built.

Y
◯

Apple introduces the first iPod in the U.S. **B**
◯

The DVD player is introduced in the U.S. **C**
◯

The first flash drive is introduced in the U.S. **R**
◯

The Sony PlayStation 2 is introduced in the U.S. **O**
◯

The first Twilight book by Stephanie Meyer is published. **T**
◯

The first HD broadcast happens in the U.S. **A**
◯

DirecTV is founded. **S**
◯

Dennis Tito, the first space tourist, goes into space. **C**
◯

The Starz movie channel is founded. **H**
◯

The WNBA is founded. **S**
◯

The first euro coins are put in circulation in Europe. **E**
◯

The first Matrix movie is released in the U.S. **L**
◯

Wikipedia is launched. **T**
◯

eBay becomes a publicly traded company. **S**
◯

(iStock)

ANSWER: ▸ □ □ □ □ □ □ □ □ □

PUZZLE #3: MAPPING YOUR MEMORY

You probably looked at a map of the United States for years while in school, but how much do you really remember about it? In each of the following questions you are given two states. Choose the correct one and circle the first letter of that answer, then unscramble the circled letters to form a word related to something smoky in Tennessee. Hint: Don't "peak" at the answer.

Which of the 48 contiguous states...

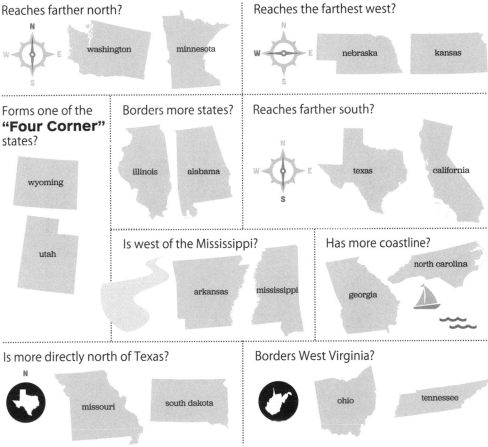

Reaches farther north?
washington   minnesota

Reaches the farthest west?
nebraska   kansas

Forms one of the **"Four Corner"** states?
wyoming
utah

Borders more states?
illinois   alabama

Reaches farther south?
texas   california

Is west of the Mississippi?
arkansas   mississippi

Has more coastline?
north carolina   georgia

Is more directly north of Texas?
missouri   south dakota

Borders West Virginia?
ohio   tennessee

ANSWER: ⬜⬜⬜⬜⬜⬜⬜⬜⬜

PUZZLE #4: COLORING OUR WORLD

You are constantly bombarded with visual stimuli in the world. In an effort to stand out, companies spend fortunes trying to choose colors that can influence your decisions, but how much attention do you really pay to the colors in their logos? Test your skills and determine the general color in each logo that is being pointed at by the white arrow. Then use the info below each logo to determine which letter of the color's name you need to use, in order, to spell a hue-morous answer.

3ʳᵈ LETTER

3ʳᵈ LETTER

2ⁿᵈ LETTER

5ᵀᴴ LETTER

1ˢᵀ LETTER

5ᵀᴴ LETTER

1ˢᵀ LETTER

1ˢᵀ LETTER

 ANSWER: ▢ ▢ ▢ ▢ ▢ ▢ ▢

PUZZLE #5: REALLY JUST WINGING IT

What the font? As a kid you may have used Wingdings to write secret encoded messages to your friends; but as an adult, those "symbol messages" might not instill the same sense of wonder in your boss. Still, there are some fun and memorable characters in the set. Examine the symbols that appear below. Take as long as you like, then turn the page and answer a few questions about them.

 **BRAIN FACT:** Having a hard time memorizing this page? Take a nap. Research has shown that sleeping before and/or after memorizing something has many significant benefits.

PUZZLE #5: REALLY JUST WINGING IT continued

Let's see how much you can remember about all those Wingdings you saw on the previous page. No worries, this is a multiple-choice test! Choose the letter of your answer. If you have all the correct answers, the letters of your choices will spell out, in order, a related message to this puzzle that completes the sentence below.

How many hands were in the picture?

A. 7   B. 8   C. 9

In which direction was the black solid arrow facing?

R. Down   E. Up   L. Right

How many of the Wingdings were also zodiac signs?

O. 1   I. 2   E. 3

How many file folders were being shown in the picture?

N. 7   A. 8   M. 9

How many file folders were shown opened?

P. 4   T. 5   L. 6

How many file folders were opening to the right?

W. 0   O. 1   V. 2

How many candles were laying on their side?

I. 3   D. 4   S. 6

Which way were the scissors opened?

E. Right   T. Up   D. Down

What was the general location of the bell in the picture?

S. Upper Left N. Upper Right W. Lower Right

I WONDER IF THEY CALL IT WINGDINGS BECAUSE YOU USUALLY HAVE A(N)...

ANSWER: ☐ ☐ ☐ ☐   ☐ ☐ ☐ ☐ .

PUZZLE #6: A CENTS ABOUT THESE THINGS

A penny for your thoughts? For this next puzzle, you will be asked questions about the 1959–2008 United States one-cent coin. Examine the two possible answers given for each question and keep track of the first letter of all the **WRONG** answers, then use those letters to spell out a big payoff.

What seven-letter word is featured on the front of a penny?

☐ AMERICA   ☐ LIBERTY

(iStock)

From your perspective, which way does the portrait face on a penny?

L OR **R**

(iStock)

On which side of the portrait does the date appear on a penny?

L 2014 R

What is the only single-letter "word" to be featured on the back of a penny?

E OR **O**

(iStock)

What is the name of the president on the front of a penny?

☐ LINCOLN
☐ WASHINGTON

Which vowel is NOT used in any word on the back of a penny?

A OR **Y**

How many total times does the word "trust" appear on a penny?

ONE OR **NONE**

Which monument is pictured on the back of a penny?

☐ LINCOLN MEMORIAL
☐ CAPITOL BUILDING

What is the approximate diameter of a penny in millimeters?

18 **19**

ANSWER: ☐ ☐ ☐ ☐ ☐ ☐ ☐

PUZZLE #7: LEFTY-RIGHTY

It's sometimes difficult to look at a photo of yourself because the image is reversed from what you typically see in a mirror. In the following logos, some of the official images have been reversed (flipped from left to right), while others have not been reversed. Can your memory help you decide which are which? Keep track of the letters that go with the reversed images to spell, in order, an appropriate phrase.

A.   C.   B.   O.

D.   U.   T.   F.

F.   A.   C.   E.

ANSWER: ☐ ☐ ☐ ☐ ☐ ☐ ☐ ☐ ☐

PUZZLE #8: ON THE PATH TO REMEMBRANCE

Finding your way around a new place can be quite a challenge, but if you pay attention, you may spot cues that will point you in a specific direction. For example, if you want to find the public transit in a big city during rush hour, just follow the hordes of people. Before you start this next puzzle, take a few minutes to memorize the picture below, trying to spot some directional cues. When you think you're ready, turn to the next page to put your memory to the test!

 BRAIN FACT: Still having a hard time memorizing stuff? Go for a run. Again and again, exercise has been shown to be beneficial for a vast array of mental functions, including memory. Your brain is part of your body, folks. A healthy body usually means a healthy brain.

PUZZLE #8: ON THE PATH TO REMEMBRANCE continued

Now that you have memorized the picture on the last page, it's time to see how you did spotting and remembering the directional cues. Starting at one of the corners of the picture that contained a triangle, draw a path through the letters that share a space with a triangle in it (moving only horizontally or vertically) until you get to another corner with a triangle in it. If you do so, you will spell out a word related to the theme of this puzzle.

ANSWER: ▢ ▢ ▢ ▢ ▢ ▢ ▢ ▢

PUZZLE #9: THE TRUE MEANING

"Memory is deceptive because it is colored by today's events." —Albert Einstein

How quickly we glance through a puzzle can determine just how much there is to actually remember. Study this page **COMPLETELY** and then turn to the next page to see just how well you did in absorbing all of the information that was laid out.

TIME

MCCALL'S

PEOPLE

WIRED

BOY'S LIFE

READER'S DIGEST

 **BRAIN FACT:** A recent study found that when primary sensory areas of the brain were more active during recall, memories were more accurate. This suggests that one way to improve the accuracy of your memories is to depend less on verbal descriptions and more on sensory imagery.

PUZZLE #__: THE _____ MEANING continued

Did you take the time to memorize the *whole* page? Let's find out with these questions. For each answer take the letter that is in parentheses and read those letters, in order, to form a phrase related to this puzzle.

According to the Brain Fact, which type of imagery improves your memory's accuracy?

SEN(S)ORY   **FAN(T)ASY**

How many of the magazine titles contained a punctuation mark?

THR(E)E   **F(O)UR**

How many lines of magazines were listed in total?

S(I)X   **S(E)VEN**

Which of these words did NOT appear in the quotation?

T(O)DAY   **Y(E)STERDAY**

What was the second word of the puzzle title?

(T)RUE   **(R)EAL**

Which magazine title was NOT listed?

ST(A)R   **WI(R)ED**

What symbol directly followed the words "Brain Fact"?

CO(L)ON   **EM D(A)SH**

What was the first name of the person quoted in the opening paragraph?

A(L)BERT   **RAN(D)OLPH**

ANSWER: ☐ ☐ ☐ ☐ ☐ ☐ ☐

BRAIN FACT: While you were trying to remember all the information on the previous page, you were relying upon two distinct memory processes: familiarity and recognition.

PUZZLE #10: MARK YOUR CALENDARS

Your days can seem to go by in the blink of an eye. So much so that you have probably glanced at a calendar and not even known the special days that have occurred. Determine which of the following U.S. holidays occurs **FIRST** in a standard calendar year with January 1 being the first day. Take the letters associated with the **EARLIER** of the two dates (which are located in the top right corner) and use them, in order, to help solve the riddle below.

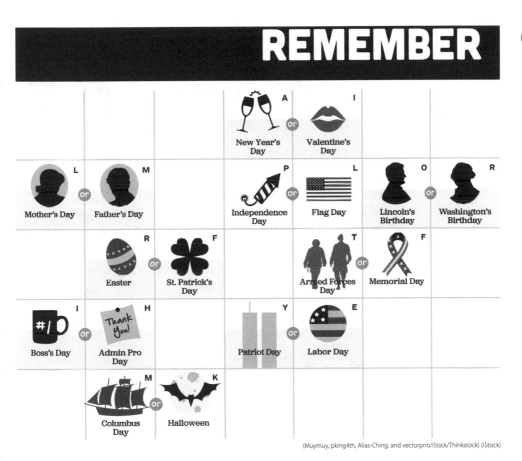

REMEMBER

	A / I New Year's Day or Valentine's Day	
L / M Mother's Day or Father's Day	P / L Independence Day or Flag Day	O / R Lincoln's Birthday or Washington's Birthday
R / F Easter or St. Patrick's Day	T / F Armed Forces Day or Memorial Day	
I / H Boss's Day or Admin Pro Day	Y / E Patriot Day or Labor Day	
M / K Columbus Day or Halloween		

(Muymuy, pking4th, Alias-Ching, and vectorprro/iStock/Thinkstock) (iStock)

HOW MANY MONTHS HAVE 28 DAYS?

ANSWER:

PUZZLE #11: ELUSIVE IDOLS

For this puzzle, take a look at all of these famous logos. Some of the logos are missing something. Can you determine which logos are missing a part? Take the letters that go with the **UNTARNISHED LOGOS** and they will spell, in order, the name of something else that has gone missing.

E.   A.   D.   R.

H.   I.   A.

T.   R.   E.   T.

MasterCard

WALT DISNEY
PICTURES

TARGET®

Tide

ANSWER: ▮ ▮ ▮ ▮ ▮ ▮

PUZZLE #12: EXCLUSIVE FRONT SEAT MEMORIES

Memories make great fodder for moviemaking. Now let's see if movies make good fodder for your memorymaking. Examine posters for movies that deal with memories in some way. In a few pages you will be asked some questions about the posters.

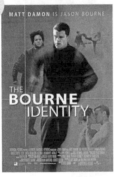

PUZZLE #13: THE TRUER MEANING

Your memory is best when it's active. If you let it become dormant, memories can fade—or worse, be blended into other memories. A few puzzles ago you were asked to look at a page of magazine titles. But then you were tricked when you were asked about other things appearing on that page. You didn't think those titles were going to go unused though, did you? Which of these titles did not appear on that page? Take the first letter of each of the new titles that appear on this page, in order, to spell a related word.

PEOPLE

TIME

MEN'S JOURNAL

INC.

SPIN

ROLLING STONE

EBONY

READER'S DIGEST

BOY'S LIFE

ALLURE

DETAILS

 ANSWER: ☐ ☐ ☐ ☐ ☐ ☐

PUZZLE #14: HMMM, CAN'T SEEM TO GET IT RIGHT

"If you tell the truth, you don't have to remember anything." —Mark Twain

Some things you take for granted because you have seen them many times. But can you remember things that are not true? Take some time to look at this list and then turn the page to test your memory.

1:   The tallest building in the U.S. capital is the **TRUMAN** Monument.

2:   *The **TYLERS** was a spin-off of the TV show All in the Family.*

3:   The name of a Grammy Award winner is **ARTHUR** Swift.

4:   The capital of Mississippi is **CARTER**.

5:   The Navigator is produced by the **POLK** Motor Company.

6:   Fox shows an animated series about the **EISENHOWERS**.

7:   William **TAFT** is on the fifty-dollar bill.

8:   A staple of many newspapers is a comic about **HARRISON** the Cat.

9:   The first vice president of the United States was **JEFFERSON**.

10: **WILSON** and **WILSON** are the makers of a children's shampoo.

11: A famous street known for advertisers in New York is **MONROE** Ave.

12: A major bean producer is **KENNEDY**'s Best.

MONROE AVE.

(iStock)

PUZZLE #14: HMMM, CAN'T SEEM TO GET IT RIGHT continued

Time to see how remembering wrong things works out for you. Match the wrong president's name on the left with the correct president's name on the right. Connecting names from one side to the other with a straight line will pass through some letters that spell, in order, a phrase related to this whole thing. Note: Some lines will go through more than one letter. Tip: Use a ruler or straight edge to help keep your lines true.

WRONG PRESIDENT	RIGHT PRESIDENT
TRUMAN	JEFFERSON
TYLER	CLEVELAND
ARTHUR	GARFIELD
CARTER	GRANT
POLK	ADAMS
EISENHOWER	TAYLOR
TAFT	LINCOLN
HARRISON	JOHNSON
JEFFERSON	MADISON
WILSON	WASHINGTON
MONROE	BUSH
KENNEDY	JACKSON

E E E I C V O T X U R E D R

ANSWER: _ _ _ _ _ _ _ _ _ _ _ _ _ _ _

FLASHBACK TO PUZZLE #12: FRONT SEAT MEMORIES

Now that the movie titles have had time to simmer in your head, let's see how well you remember them. Let's keep it simple with a true or false quiz of your memory. Take the letter next to each puzzle to spell out, in order, a phrase related to the puzzle.

	TRUE	or FALSE
Adam Sandler's movie is next to Leonardo DiCaprio's.	E	A
Adam Sandler is on the right side of his movie poster.	I	N
Four movies have the word "THE" in their title.	T	S
The middle row is in reverse alphabetical order by title.	W	L
The poster for *Memento* lists two actors by name on it.	P	E
Two movie posters have people kissing or ready to kiss.	R	O
The Matt Damon movie has the most people shown on it.	N	E
At least one poster shows a musical instrument.	M	L
At least three posters have the same person shown more than once.	E	L
The Bourne movie shown is the first in the series.	M	R
Only one movie has a character from the movie in the title.	S	B
Only one poster has no actor names on it.	E	O
The first row is in order of when the film was released.	N	R

ANSWER: ▢ ▢ ▢ ▢ ▢ ▢   ▢ ▢ ▢ ▢ ▢ ▢

PUZZLE #15: DOES IT GO ANY HIGHER?

On a daily basis you consume a vast amount of information. Try to imagine how many numbers that you absorb in a single day. Is it in the hundreds? Thousands? Millions? Out of all those numbers can you recall some pretty well-known ones? In the following list there is a fact with a number in it, and it's wrong. Decide if that number is too high or too low to be that number. Take the letter that goes with the answers that are too high. In doing so you will spell out, in order, a suitable phrase.

I	150:	Maximum characters in a tweet on Twitter.
N	48:	"The answer to life, the universe and everything."
T	86:	Elements on the periodic table.
F	12:	Number of fluid ounces in a cup.
O	24:	Cost of a normal U.S. stamp, in cents, in 1990.
I	17:	Herbs and spices in the original KFC flavor.
C	16:	Legal voting age in the U.S.
A	10:	Speed limit in a school zone.
R	8:	Zeros in one trillion.
N	59:	Number of Heinz "varieties" listed on their products.
I	45:	The number president that Barack Obama is.
A	72:	Quarters in $20 USD.
T	11:	Number of Harry Potter movies starring Daniel Radcliffe.
N	20:	Number of seasons that *The Simpsons* has been on.
C	3:	Number of Great Lakes in the U.S.
Y	55:	Cards in a standard poker-sized playing deck.
D	150:	Countries in the world.

(Emir Simsek and Sofia Vlasiuk/ iStock/Thinkstock)

ANSWER: ▪ ▪ ▪ ▪ ▪ ▪ ▪

PUZZLE #16: A SEQUEL TO REMEMBER

The power of a plural. You were asked to memorize a list of memory-related movies in a previous puzzle. You were also told that you would be reminded "over a few pages." Can you remember the order of the movies? Take the indicated letter of the indicated word of each title and unscramble those letters to spell out a related phrase.

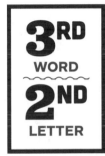

ANSWER:

PUZZLE #17: SPORTING A NEW MEMORY

What is your "goal" in trying to remember facts? Trying to "catch" up with knowledge? Go ahead and "kick" these questions around for a bit. "Knock out" the answers in the grid by circling the letters next to the answer numbers. Use the resulting letters to spell a sporty phrase.

 Number of periods in NHL hockey, no overtime.

Number of outs in a regulation game of baseball. No extra innings.

Time in seconds on an NBA shot clock.

Minute warning at the end of each half in the NFL.

 Laps in the Indy 500.

 Minutes in an NFL football quarter.

 Total regulation time in minutes of a World Cup soccer match

 Length in meters of the men's Olympic hurdles.

 Players allowed on defense in one play of the NFL.

 Points needed to win a game in tennis.

The number of strikes it takes to score 300 in one round of bowling.

 Number of total yards in length of a NFL football field, including end zones.

40 W	12 I	2 N	20 R	10 S
75 E	120 S	15 T	5 U	16 C
30 H	200 A	125 D	4 N	18 T
60 B	3 R	100 O	54 E	45 N
90 P	21 C	50 I	11 L	13 E
220 N	24 A	70 B	80 L	110 Y

 The number of holes in a standard round of golf.

ANSWER:

PUZZLE #18: PLANES, TRAINS, AND AUTOMOBILES

In a previous puzzle you were asked to remember U.S. geography, but now it's time to test your knowledge of Europe! Shown below are 11 European countries. Each has two country names on it, but only one is correct. Use the correct name and the information below to learn which letters you will need to extract from the country names in order to spell an eleven-lettered word related to a way of traveling Europe.

The country's name is...

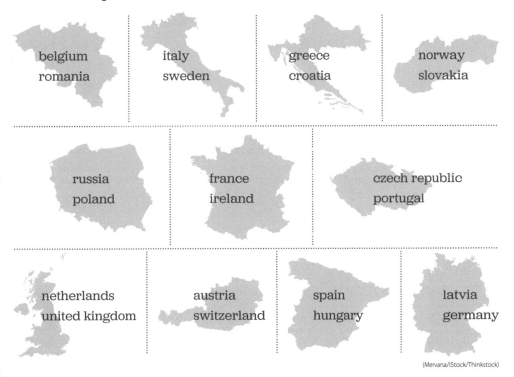

belgium
romania

italy
sweden

greece
croatia

norway
slovakia

russia
poland

france
ireland

czech republic
portugal

netherlands
united kingdom

austria
switzerland

spain
hungary

latvia
germany

(Mervana/iStock/Thinkstock)

EXTRACT THESE LETTERS, IN ORDER, FROM THE CORRECT COUNTRY NAMES:

1 3 1 6 1 3 1 7 6 5 1

ANSWER: ▢ ▢ ▢ ▢ ▢ ▢ ▢ ▢ ▢ ▢ ▢

Here's a different response letter. This time it sounds quite the opposite. There are seven words that are direct opposites from those in the letter before. Take the first letter of each of those words from the original message, in order, to spell out a phrase that describes the original message.

I must take this time to accept the invitation you sent me this week. I am happy to be invited and I have even narrowed down a time for the meeting. I am always glad to be of company and will be present for our meeting. I see no question why I could not make it this time, our being only miles apart.
—Patrick

flip! **flip!**

I must take this time to decline the invitation that you sent me this week. I found it odd that you would ask me to widen my view about you this time. I would never think that such past events would lead to this, but now that you have my answer the chance of us getting together is impossible.
—Patrick

next step.

only to be halfway there and realize you truly don't. Take a look at the following paragraph and take some time to memorize it. Once you are ready, flip the page over to reveal your

How many times have you been given directions to a place and think you have it locked in,

PUZZLE # 19: TWO-SIDED

PUZZLE #20: INITIAL FEEDBACK

HOMES. Huron, Ontario, Michigan, Erie, Superior. Mnemonics can be a great way to make memorizing a list of items much easier. But what good is a mnemonic if you can't remember what it's supposed to stand for? Examine these logos, then after the next puzzle, see how well you've done on this abbreviated test.

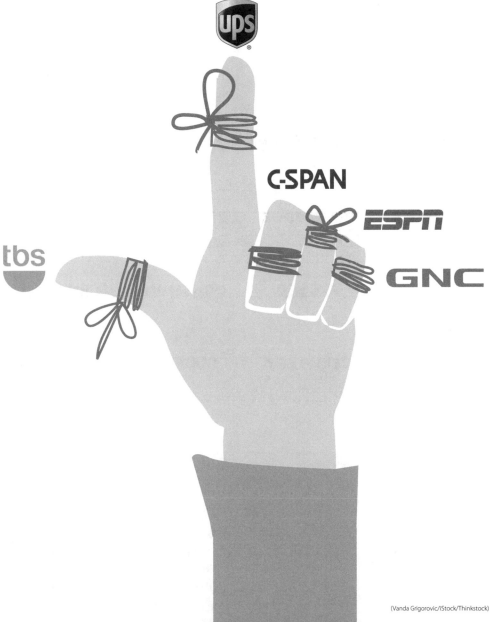

(Vanda Grigorovic/iStock/Thinkstock)

PUZZLE #21: MISSPELLED OR MISPELLED?

One of the first times your memory was tested was probably when you first took home a list of spelling words to memorize. Now that you have spell-check AND auto-correct options, how many of those words do you actually remember? Let's find out. In the following list there are words spelled correctly and some that are not. Take the first letter of the words spelled correctly, in order, to form a suitable phrase.

DUMBELL	INOCULATE	SIEZE	BOOKKEEPER
MINNISCULE	EMBARRASS	SEPERATE	FIERY
ACIDENTLY	PRIVILEDGE	OCCURRENCE	MISPELL
REPETITION	EXCEED	OCASSION	EQUIPTMENT
MILLENIUM	CEMATERY	SUCEDE	EXHILARATE

ANSWER: ▢ ▢ ▢ ▢ ▢ ▢ ▢

BRAIN FACT: Evidence suggests that your impressive ability to read comes from a region in your occipito-temporal cortex called the visual word form area. In studies, this area activates whenever people are reading, including some blind people reading Braille.

PUZZLE #20: INITIAL FEEDBACK continued

Did you memorize the logos AND what they stood for? Examine this new set of logos. Determine which logos share at least one word with the logos on the previous page of the puzzle. Some logos on the previous page will match more than one on this page. Take the initial letter of the logos that do NOT share a word with any logos on the previous page, then unscramble those letters to spell a word related to information.

ANSWER: ▶ □ □ □ □

🧠 **BRAIN FACT:** The puzzle above requires visual object recognition, a process that depends mostly on activity in the inferotemporal (i.e., the lower section of the temporal) cortex. This brain area is where all the information about the visual aspects of an object combines.

PUZZLE #22: THE TRILOGY CONCLUDES

"A few pages." That's what it said. This time you are working with new movies starring the same lead actors as before. Place the movies on this page in order of their release date. Then, using the lead actors as your guide, find the letters you will need to unscramble the answer on this page in the titles of the corresponding movies you were asked to memorize in the previous memory puzzle.

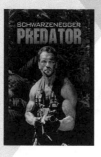

1ˢᵗ Clue: **2ⁿᵈ Letter, 2ⁿᵈ Word**

2ⁿᵈ Clue: **3ʳᵈ Letter, 2ⁿᵈ Word**

3ʳᵈ Clue: **2ⁿᵈ Letter, 2ⁿᵈ Word**

4ᵗʰ Clue: **3ʳᵈ Letter, 1ˢᵗ Word**

5ᵗʰ Clue: **6ᵗʰ Letter, 2ⁿᵈ Word**

6ᵗʰ Clue: **3ʳᵈ Letter, 1ˢᵗ Word**

7ᵗʰ Clue: **5ᵗʰ Letter, 1ˢᵗ Word**

8ᵗʰ Clue: **4ᵗʰ Letter, 2ⁿᵈ Word**

(bubaone/iStock/Thinkstock)

 ANSWER:

PUZZLE #23: LOGO A GO-GO

As mentioned before, advertisers want to get their product or business ingrained in your mind. Well, let's see how that worked for you. The following memory puzzle has everything to do with the logos you have seen in the previous memory puzzles. The movie posters are not included. Take the letter associated with your choice to spell a very relevant phrase.

1 Which of the following logos appeared first in a puzzle?
F. Lego　　　T. Wikipedia　　　C. Internet Explorer

2 Which of these animals appears first?
E. Fox　　　O. Horse　　　R. Lion

3 How many logos feature the number "1" in them?
A. 0　　　C. 1　　　E. 2

4 How many automobile manufacturer logos were seen?
U. 3　　　T. 4　　　A. 5

5 How many logos featured a person wearing glasses?
S. 1　　　N. 2　　　E. 3

6 Which logo with three faces in it was featured?
T. PBS　　　I. Pep Boys　　　G. The Girl Scouts of America

7 How many logos contain (or should contain) a human shape?
A. 5　　　R. 6　　　O. 7

8 How many logos featured five-pointed stars?
N. 0　　　O. 1　　　C. 2

9 Which of these first appeared in a puzzle? A person wearing a:
U. Crown　　　C. Bow　　　A. Hat

10 Which of these letters appears the least in all of the logo images?
P. "M"　　　S. "T"　　　K. "C"

ANSWER: ▮ ▮ ▮ ▮ ▮　▮ ▮ ▮ ▮

PUZZLE #24: ALL OVER THE PLACE

In recalling images, you can easily overlap thought, especially when things closely resemble each other. Memorize the following images. When you are finished, rotate the page and answer the question at hand.

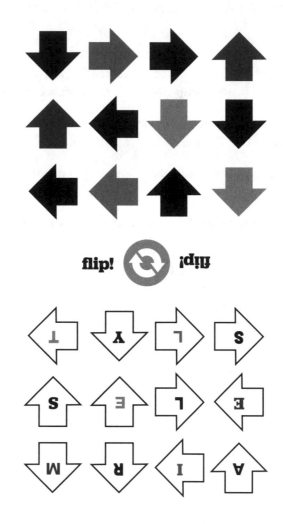

flip! 🔄 ¡dıɟ

˙noʎ ʇou ʎllnɟǝdoɥ puɐ ǝlzznd ǝɥʇ oʇ pǝʇɐlǝɹ pɹoʍ ɐ ʇno llǝds oʇ ǝƃuɐɥɔ ʇou pᴉp sǝuo ɥɔᴉɥʍ ǝuᴉɯɹǝʇǝ⦿ ˙uoᴉʇɔǝɹᴉp ɹǝɥʇouɐ uᴉ ǝɔɐɟ oʇ ǝɹnʇɔᴉd lɐuᴉƃᴉɹo ǝɥʇ ɯoɹɟ pǝɹǝʇlɐ uǝǝq ǝʌɐɥ sʍoɹɹɐ ǝɯoS ˙ʇno puᴉɟ s,ʇǝ˥ ¿noʎ ɥʇᴉʍ ssǝɯ sʍoɹɹɐ ǝɥʇ pᴉ⦿

 ANSWER: ☐ ☐ ☐ ☐ ☐ ☐ ☐

PUZZLE #25: HAVE YOU EARNED YOUR TITLE?

You have reached the summit of your journey. It's time for your final exam. All the answers are in the form of a fill-in-the-blank. Good luck! Hint: After you remember all the titles you "earned," take the first letter of each answer to reveal one final message.

memory
MASTER

The .... Concludes

Does it Go Any ....

.... OVER THE PLACE

Sporting A .... Memory

Placement is ....

A .... TO REMEMBER

Initial ....

Coloring .... World

LEFTY– ....

.... -Sided

.... , Can't Seem to Get it Right

.... IDOLS

The Truer ....

.... Front Seat Memories

.... YOUR MEMORY

.... the Path to Remembrance

.... Just Winging It

.... –ISH

ANSWER:

⬛ ⬛ ⬛ ⬛ ⬛ ⬛   ⬛ ⬛   ⬛ ⬛ ⬛

⬛ ⬛ ⬛ ⬛ ⬛

FOR THOSE WHO STILL HAVE QUESTIONS

➤➤ ➤➤ ➤➤

VISUAL PERCEPTION ANSWERS

1. **A.** A fly in the ointment, **B.** Lying under oath, **C.** Put on weight, **D.** Tulips

2. **A.** Alcatraz/California, **B.** Guggenheim Museum/New York, **C.** Plymouth Rock/Massachusetts, **D.** Mr. Rushmore, South Dakota, **E.** Devil's Tower/Wyoming, **F.** Churchill Downs/Kentucky (home of the Kentucky Derby), **G.** Wrigley Field/Illinois, **H.** The Alamo/Texas

3. GUMbo, CABbage, Nectarines (NECKtarines), PUMPkin, Peaches (Pches), **and** Brownie (BrowKNEE)

4. **A.** Foreign language, **B.** Two left feet, **C.** What goes up, must come down, **D.** Once upon a time

5. Brainwave, Cheesecake, Fingernail, Rattlesnake, Teaspoon, **and** Football

6. **A.** Mixed blessings, **B.** Keep it under your hat, **C.** I have no idea, **D.** Banana split

7. **GAME A. Baseball positions:** Batter, Catcher, Pitcher. **GAME B. Dances:** Swing, Salsa, Charleston. **GAME C. Jacks:** Jack o' lantern, Union Jack, Jackass.

8. **A.** Marlboro cigarettes, **B.** Morton salt, **C.** Planter's peanuts, **D.** Mr. Clean, **E.** Cracker Jack, **F.** Betty Crocker mixes, **G.** Chef Boyardee spaghetti and pizza, **H.** Sun-Maid raisins, **I.** Brawny paper towels, **J.** Bazooka bubble gum, **K.** Chicken of the Sea tuna, **L.** Burger King

9. MosCOW, AFGHANistan, BRAzil, CANada, TurKEY, JaPAN, BAGhdad, FLAGStaff, **and** VANcouver

10. **A.** Too little, too late, **B.** Halfhearted, **C.** Sign on the dotted line, **D.** Painless operation

11. WAVElength, FootNOTES, DrawBRIDGE, ThumbNAIL, STARvation, TuLIPS, Oboe (oBOW), EGGnog, **and** CourtSHIP

12. Sundial, Topknot, Crab apple, Inchworm, Drumsticks, **and** Shoehorn

13. **GAME A. Geometrical Shapes:** Bermuda Triangle, Times Square, Oval Office. **GAME B. Nationalities:** English muffin, Chinese checkers, French fries. **GAME C. Animals:** Baseball bat, Hot dog, Michael J. Fox. **GAME D. Alphabet Letters:** I (Eye), P (Pea), Q (Cue).

14. PLUMber, Pilot (PIElot), JocKEY, FireFIGHTER, Pharmacist (FARMacist), LOCKSmith, CARpenter, TEAcher, **and** Florist (FLOORist)

15. **GAME A. D** is the Odd Man Out. It is a picture of Radar O'Reilly, a character from the television series *M*A*S*H*. All of the others are fictional captains (Cap'n Crunch, Captain Kirk, Captain Hook). **GAME B. B** is the Odd Man Out. All of the other pictures

contain items with eyes (potato, hurricane, needle). **GAME C. C** is the Odd Man Out. All of the other pictures represent types of cookies (Girl Scout cookies, pinwheel cookies, butter cookies). **GAME D. A** is the Odd Man Out. It is a picture of Tom Cruise. All of the others are actors/directors who have the same first and last initial (Robert Redford, Steven Spielberg, Alan Alda).

16. Firecracker, Raincheck, Carpool, Handbook, Buttermilk, **and** Starfish

17. Bee + four + GOD + (web - B) + R + (wall – w) + (E + (quilt – T) + E) + Y's + (hand – H) + (E + (quilt – T) + E) + (fool + ISH). ("Before God we are all equally wise and equally foolish." —Albert Einstein)

18. Watchdog, Spring water, Shoe tree, Catfish, Sawhorse, **and** Bullpen

19.

ITEM LIST: leopard, lemur, ladder, lightning, lamp, lizard (X2), leaf, lion, Liberty Bell, label, lamb, lock, lighthouse, luggage, leash, log, lantern, lemon, **and** laptop

20. A. Oprah Winfrey, **B.** Angelina Jolie, **C.** Jane Fonda, **D.** Michelle Obama, **E.** Beyoncé, **F.** Gwyneth Paltrow

21. (QU + (bucket - buck)) ׀ (pea + PLE) + (H + (calf - C)) + THE + ((cloud - C) + EST) + (M + (nines - N)). ("Quiet people have the loudest minds." — Stephen Hawking)

22.

ITEM LIST: ribbon, reindeer, rat, rollerskate, rosary, rocket, radio, rabbit (X3), rectangle, rattle, rake, rope, raindrop, ring, rattlesnake, radish, rifle, ravioli, rooster, radiator, rice, roach, raven, runner (X2), rhino, rocking horse, rock, reptile, race car, rose, robot, **and** rodeo boot.

23. A. Johnny Depp, **B.** Anderson Cooper, **C.** Brad Pitt, **D.** Prince William, **E.** Will Smith, **F.** George Clooney

24. (TH + hose) + (hoop - P) + (D + knife + RE + (dumbbell - BELL)) + two + (mother - M + S) + (D + (surfboard - BOARD)) + IT + knot + four + (TH + hem + S + elves). ("Those who deny freedom to others deserve it not for themselves." —Abraham Lincoln)

25. Phonographs (1877), modern typewriters (1867), telephones (1876), *Harper's Bazaar* magazine (1867), radios (1890s), zippers (1913), Wright Brothers' plane (or models of their plane; 1900s), Zachary Taylor (November 24, 1784–July 9, 1850), modern yo-yos (1928), "Adventures of Tom Sawyer" book (1876), **and** vacuum cleaners (1901). (**NOT:** parachutes (1470s), lawn mowers (1827), cameras (1826), Abraham Lincoln (February 12, 1809–April 15, 1865), **or** telescopes (1608).)

WORD SKILLS ANSWERS

1. **A.** Noon, Nest, True, Even, Next, Tent, Tilt, Tuna, Aura, Able, Ever, Ruin, Neat, Torn
   B. Smash, Honk, Knit, Tar, Ramp, Poke, Elm, Mount, Tin, Nets, Self, Flop, Pass

2. **A.** Eddy, Yell, Latte, Error, Riddle, Endless, Scoot, Thrill, Loon, Noon, Nook, Knee
   B. Huff, Fret, Tutor, Rob, Bash, Hound, Dwell, Lead, Dive, Envy, Yap, Pilot, Throw, Wish

3. **A.** Access, Soda, Above, Exam, Mayor, Ruby, Yodel, Lady, Yoga, Awake, Extra
   B. Sight, Taste, Elbow, World, Dance, Eaten, Named, Deuce, Exits

4. **A.** Laughing all the way to the bank. **B.** Put your money where your mouth is.

5. **A.** Absence makes the heart grow fonder. **B.** Sitting on the edge of your seat.

6. **A.** Time flies when you are having fun. **B.** Diamonds are a girl's best friend.

7. **A.** Playing both sides of the fence. **B.** Birds of a feather flock together.

8. **A.** Two heads are better than one. **B.** Have your cake and eat it too.

9. **A.** Cleveland, Berlin, Anchorage, Lincoln, London, Madrid, Phoenix, Glasgow, Sydney, Honolulu **B.** Umpire, Grounder, Triple, Season, Dugout, Strike, Pitcher, Uniform, Manager, Outfield

10. **A.** Jefferson, Truman, Madison, Clinton, Johnson, Kennedy, Garfield, Carter, Roosevelt, Harding **B.** Pelican, Parakeet, Thrush, Mallard, Nuthatch, Albatross, Cuckoo, Pigeon, Rooster, Falcon

11. **A.** Sundae, Custard, Toffee, Cookie, Brownie, Gelato, Truffle, Cupcake, Macaroon, Strudel **B.** Recliner, Couch, Daybed, Bookcase, Armoire, Chaise, Ottoman, Hutch, Hammock, Waterbed

12. **A.** Cherry, Orange, Banana, Guava, Persimmon, Currant, Pineapple, Lychee, Kumquat, Apricot **B.** McKinley, Klondike, Whitney, Olympus, Whistler, Helens, Everest, Greenhorn, Bachelor, Vesuvius

13. **A.** *Superman, Superbad, Predator, Gremlins, Godzilla, Fantasia, Twilight*
    B. Lisbon, London, Athens, Warsaw, Vienna, Madrid

14. **A.** Raccoon, Leopard, Buffalo, Caribou, Warthog, Gorilla, Hamster
    B. Awesome, Careful, Offbeat, Prudent, Stylish, Thirsty

15. **A.** Hydrogen, Titanium, Nitrogen, Platinum, Tungsten, Fluorine, Chromium
    B. Denver, Atlanta, Topeka, Albany, Boston, Lansing

16. **A.** Hot, Taxing, Gifted, Decent, Ticklish
    B. Retina, Absorb, Bikini, Iodine, Export, Thinly, Yellow, Winter

17. A. Apricot, Tomato, Onion, Nectarine, Eggplant, Turnip, Papaya
B. Turtle, Elephant, Tiger, Rabbit

18. A. Ginger, Rosemary, Yarrow, Watercress, Saffron, Nutmeg
B. Dribble, Eddy, Yell, Lesson, Noodle, Egg, Greed

19. A. Tackle, Error, Rush, Helmet, Toboggan, Net
B. Rumble, Escort, Traffic, Central, Lion, Number

20. A.   **B.**

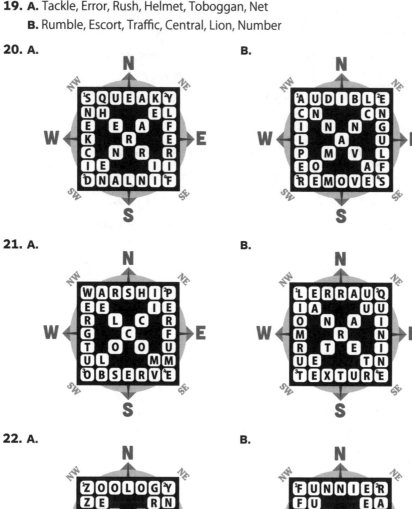

21. A.   **B.**

22. A.   **B.**

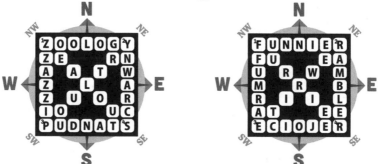

23. A.

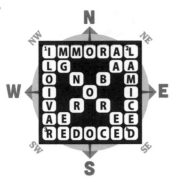

B.

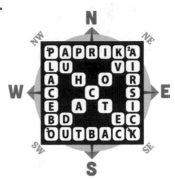

24. A.

U	J	O	S	T
M	F	R	N	O
B	O	D	Y	I
U	R	N	A	S
P	S	E	C	E

B.

A	N	T	E	D
H	N	A	C	A
C	E	F	I	S
R	X	U	R	B
E	M	S	H	U

25. A.

M	A	G	M	A
E	D	O	I	D
N	I	D	G	E
I	S	R	I	G
C	E	N	G	A

B.

I	M	P	L	O
R	P	A	D	C
E	D	E	K	K
R	N	D	W	A
R	A	S	Q	U

26. A.

E	N	T	H	U
E	N	D	O	S
B	L	G	W	I
O	U	T	S	A
G	T	T	O	N

B.

Z	O	P	A	M
A	R	E	I	P
R	A	G	P	H
T	M	E	R	L
E	M	P	T	E

27. Chrysler, Cheers, Facebook, Hudson, Rolex, Calcium, Mantle, United, Ninety, Nile, India

28. Toronto, Shelley, Aruba, Bering, Mercury, Mustang, Proton, Abacus, Anaconda, Steel, Peru, Dime

29. Lucas, Rugby, Amsterdam, Pacino, Parton, *Peanuts*, Mexico, Amazon, Morse, Galileo, Llama

CRITICAL THINKING ANSWERS

1.

2	6	5	4	1	1	2	1
4	0	2	6	5	4	2	3
5	3	4	4	2	0	3	1
1	6	6	5	1	5	0	4
0	0	3	0	2	5	0	6
0	3	1	5	6	2	2	4
1	6	6	3	3	4	3	5

2.

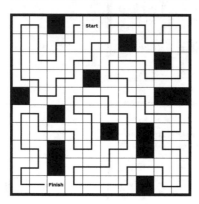

3. "Some books are undeservedly forgotten; none are undeservedly remembered."
(Wystan Hugh Auden)

4.

H	O	I	S	T	E	D		E	M	C	E	E
O		N		H		Y		L		A		L
K	U	D	Z	U		E	J	E	C	T	E	D
U		E		N		V		C				E
M	I	X	E	D	M	E	T	A	P	H	O	R
		E		E		D		T				L
B	U	S		R	H	I	N	O		F	L	Y
E				S		T		R		O		
Q	U	I	E	T	A	S	A	M	O	U	S	E
U		M		R				U		L		P
E	R	A	S	U	R	E		S	E	T	T	O
S		G		C		B		I		I		X
T	W	E	A	K		B	A	C	K	P	A	Y

[1] I	[2] N	[3] Y	[4] S	[5] R	[6] O	[7] U	[8] E	[9] D	[10] V	[11] J	[12] Z	[13] X
[14] H	[15] F	[16] B	[17] M	[18] T	[19] P	[20] C	[21] L	[22] Q	[23] A	[24] K	[25] G	[26] W

5.

	Betty	Cathy	Ellen	Jack	Chris
Monday	JOSH NOSE HONKING	ALICE TUMBLING	BEN FIRE JUGGLING	MIKE PLATE SPINNING	HEATHER LION TAMING
Tuesday	ALICE LION TAMING	MIKE NOSE HONKING	HEATHER PLATE SPINNING	BEN TUMBLING	JOSH FIRE JUGGLING
Wednesday	BEN PLATE SPINNING	HEATHER FIRE JUGGLING	ALICE NOSE HONKING	JOSH LION TAMING	MIKE TUMBLING
Thursday	HEATHER TUMBLING	JOSH PLATE SPINNING	MIKE LION TAMING	ALICE FIRE JUGGLING	BEN NOSE HONKING
Friday	MIKE FIRE JUGGLING	BEN LION TAMING	JOSH TUMBLING	HEATHER NOSE HONKING	ALICE PLATE SPINNING

6.

Crossword grid:

```
P I X I E   A D M I T   S H A D Y
I     A   R     E   S E   D
Z   S S N O W F L A K E E   I
Z S U T M ■ L ■ S   D R E A M
A M P L E A C U T E   M U   A
  E R   T       M O N   I
J R E L I T E     O     Z
F N G   A   N A M E N A M E S
A M O N G B   C   Y   I ■ O
N ■ V   M L   T   B A S I C
S H A K E A L E G   A   T   K
Y   I   C R U M B   B   L S
E   N   R     Y   E
N A F   S W E E P   T E T R A
A M B E R W ■ P ■ I   E   O   L
  I A R A B E S Q U E E   I
  D M M       U       T   A
P I E C E   I M A G E   H U M U S
```

7.

A	E	O	I	C	T	U	N	D
I	U	C	N	O	D	E	T	A
T	N	D	E	A	U	I	C	O
D	I	N	A	U	O	T	E	C
E	C	T	D	I	N	A	O	U
U	O	A	T	E	C	D	I	N
C	A	I	U	N	E	O	D	T
O	T	E	C	D	A	N	U	I
N	D	U	O	T	I	C	A	E

(Bonus: ACDEINOTU spells "auctioned," "cautioned," and "education.")

8.

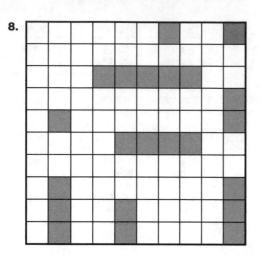

9. ABHJPW, CDGILO, EFQRSY, KNTUVX

10. A. Uncool, Thrush, Afraid, Sesame, Loofah, Object, Piglet, Byword. **B.** Noun, Cord, Ruby, Pith, Sect, Meet, Loaf, Glob, Jerk, Rash, Idol, Woof. **BONUS:** Noah's Ark

11.

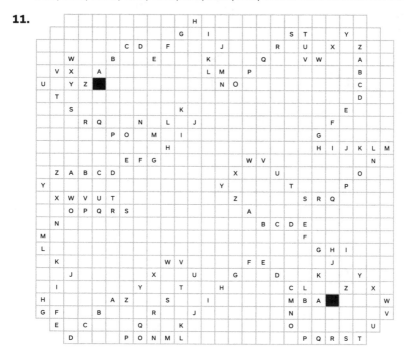

12. GUEST ROOM: 3 bulbs, 15, 25, and 60 watts, **LIVING ROOM:** 6 bulbs, 15, 15, 15, 15, 15, and 25 watts, **OFFICE:** 5 bulbs, 15, 15, 15, 15, and 40 watts, **BATHROOM:** 2 bulbs, 40 and 60 watts, **CYNTHIA'S BEDROOM:** 4 bulbs, 25 watts each, **KITCHEN:** 2 bulbs, 75 and 25 watts

13. 1. Precarious, **2.** Anaïs Nin, **3.** Wiseacre, **4.** Hierarchy, **5.** Washed up, **6.** Phone tag, **7.** High-tech, **8.** Twin Cities, **9.** Headhunter, **10.** Penny-ante.

"There are years when nothing happens and years in which centuries happen." (Carlos Fuentes)

14.

```
P U M P     M O J O
    I     E   A       N O R M
M U C H   E   M       L     A
A   K     L E A F   Y       N
A         D       I   M A Y O
L O A F   G       N         P
    L A Z Y   K N I T       U
K I W I           U F O S
N     P O U T   J A M B
O         H   I   A C H E
B I R D   A   N         A
  A   D   W A X Y     E   V
  M   O   Q     O   O B O E
  B I K E   U   G       B
    S O F A   A X I S
```

15.

4	6	4	5	2	5	1	4	4
1	2	2	1	6	6	3	5	0
3	3	0	0	3	2	3	0	6
6	1	2	6	0	1	1	5	6
1	4	3	4	3	4	2	4	5
2	0	5	3	2	0	0	1	5

The 5-6 is the missing tile.

16.

Z	I	N	C	O	X	I	D	E		M	O	T	H	S
I		O		R		V		M		I		R		K
P	A	T	S	D	R	Y		P	A	C	K	A	G	E
P		E		E				T			I			D
Y	A	P		R	E	A	D	Y		J	U	N	T	A
		A			W			O		E				D
R	A	D	I	O		A	D	D		K	N	E	A	D
E				F	A	R		E	K	E				D
Q	U	A	F	F		E	B	B		R	U	P	E	E
U		R		E				U			R			
I	N	C	U	R		D	I	G	I	T		O	R	B
S		H			W			U			F			L
I	M	I	T	A	T	E		A	I	R	L	I	N	E
T		V		N		E		P		B		T		E
E	L	E	G	Y		B	O	T	T	O	M	S	U	P

¹S	²X	³D	⁴L	⁵I	⁶Y	⁷W	⁸Z	⁹Q	¹⁰R	¹¹P	¹²G	¹³U
¹⁴N	¹⁵H	¹⁶B	¹⁷C	¹⁸A	¹⁹F	²⁰E	²¹V	²²T	²³O	²⁴J	²⁵M	²⁶K

17.

18.

```
      D A M   E B B
    S O C K   S E A M
  R I G H T A S R A I N
M O M M Y   L A G   D O E
P A P A   S L Y   A D D S
H D L   S K I   A R L E S
  E A S Y A S P I E
B A S I N   N E E   C T R
B R I M   I C E   S L A B
C A M   O N E   D H A B I
  B O L D A S B R A S S
  N O O N   O A R S
    P R E   A M P
```

19. "No one gossips about other people's secret virtues." (Bertrand Russell)

20. **WORDS:** Sugar rush, Headphones, Out of sight, Escrow, Store, Hoot, Indeed, North, El Greco, Bottle cap, On the nose, Yemen.

TRIVIA: This alter ego of cartoon superhero Underdog destroys telephone booths when he changes into costume.

TRIVIA ANSWER, READING DOWN: Shoeshine Boy

21.

```
B O S C   D A M S   M I S E R
A R E A   O L E O   I N T R O
S C A R   G O R Y   S T O O L
H A R A N G U E   B L O N D E
    F E E D   B E E   Y E S
C A R E E R   P E T A L
A L E   D E F E R   D A W N S
S L A W   L A T E R   P A I L
H Y P E D   U T T E R   I C E
    E A R L Y   D E N T E D
S E T   R A T   C O L A
C R E A K Y   P O L Y G L O T
E R A S E   H I D E   G A V E
N O S E S   O P E N   E V E N
T R E A T   W E S T   D A R T
```

TO BE UNDERSTOOD, THE QUOTATION MUST BE READ BACKWARD: "Mirrors should reflect a little before throwing back images." (Jean Cocteau)

22.

T	E	D	N	M	I	S	X	U
X	I	M	U	S	T	D	N	E
U	S	N	D	X	E	I	T	M
M	X	E	T	I	N	U	D	S
I	T	U	S	D	M	X	E	N
D	N	S	X	E	U	T	M	I
E	U	X	M	T	S	N	I	D
N	M	T	I	U	D	E	S	X
S	D	I	E	N	X	M	U	T

DEIMNSTUX spells MIXED NUTS.

23.

I	M	A	M			E	T	R	E		S	E	N	T
M	E	M	O		S	L	E	P	T		A	V	O	W
A	S	S	N		M	E	X	I	C	O	C	I	T	Y
	A	T	T	R	A	C	T			G	R	A	I	L
	E	R	E	C	T		A	T	L	A	N	T	A	
S	T	R	E	A	K		S	P	I	E	L			
P	E	D	A	L		S	E	A	L			B	U	T
O	R	A	L		S	C	O	R	E		H	A	S	H
T	A	M			T	A	U	T		T	E	R	S	E
		S	K	I	L	L		V	E	L	C	R	O	
A	N	T	W	E	R	P		S	E	N	S	E		
L	I	V	E	R			F	E	R	T	I	L	E	
L	O	S	A	N	G	E	L	E	S		N	O	T	E
I	B	E	T		A	W	A	K	E		K	N	O	T
N	E	T	S		P	E	W	S		I	A	N	S	

THE NINE CITIES IN THIS GRID WERE ALL HOSTS OF THE SUMMER OLYMPICS:
Antwerp (1920), Amsterdam (1928), Los Angeles (1932 & 1984), Helsinki (1952),
Mexico City (1968), Montreal (1976), Seoul (1988), Barcelona (1992), Atlanta (1996).

24. "If I've told you once, I've told you a thousand times: resist hyperbole." (William Safire)

25.

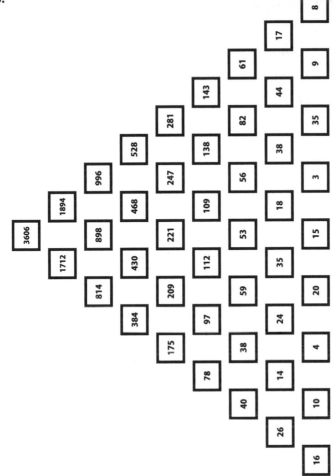

26. ACIJRT, BFMNOQ, DKSUXY, EHLPVW

27. "Prose is words in their best order; poetry is the best words in their best order." (Samuel Taylor Coleridge)

28. **1001:** Chris, Beech Baron, autopilot upgrade, white

1002: Paul, Aeronca Champ, replacement of vacuum pump, green with blue stripes

1003: Chuck, Mooney M20J, radio upgrade, blue with red tail

1004: Nellie, Piper Archer, replacement of landing gear motors, green with black wings

1005: Harriet, Cessna Skyhawk, resealing of fuel tanks, yellow

1006: Lane, Cirrus SR22, complete engine overhaul, red with white stripes

COORDINATION ANSWERS

1. **N/A**

2. **N/A**

3. BISON (or rather, "Bye, son")

4. Amalgam

5. Fresh

6. Well played

7. Milton Glaser

8. **N/A**

9. **N/A**

10. **(SEE PAGE 185)**

11. Features

12. Handy trick

13. **(SEE PAGE 186)**

14. Intellect

15. Fitness

16. Clever

17. **(SEE PAGE 185)**

18. Fission chips

19. Black

20. Curious

21. **(SEE PAGE 186)**

22–23. **N/A**

24–26. **N/A**

27. Noggin

28. Jargon

29. "You have reached the last page. Congrats on being awesome."

10.

17.

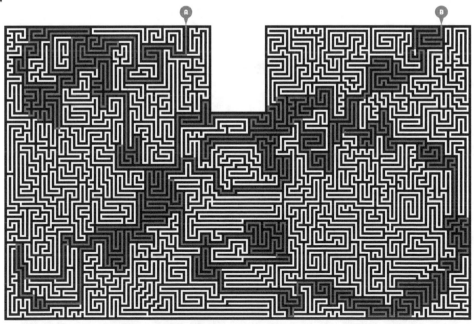

13.

21.

MEMORY ANSWERS

1. CTRL ALT DEL

2. Crashless

3. Mountains

4. Rainbows (PuRple, orAnge, pInk, greeN, Blue, yellOw, White, **and** Silver)

5. Arial View

6. Allowance (The first letter of all the incorrect answers)

7. About Face (The Pepsi, GE and Twitter logos are not reversed)

8. Traveling

9. See It All

10. All of Them

11. Earhart (DQ is missing its top swoosh, Disney is missing its flags, Wikipedia is missing its symbols **and** United Way is missing a person)

12. Aisle Remember

13. Misread

14. Executive Order (Truman → Washington, Tyler → Jefferson, Arthur → Taylor, Carter → Jackson, Polk → Lincoln, Eisenhower → Cleveland, Taft → Grant, Harrison → Garfield, Jefferson → Adams, Wilson → Johnson, Monroe → Madison, **and** Kennedy → Bush)

15. Infinity

16. Rebooted

17. Instant Replay

18. Backpacking

19. Down Pat (Decline, Odd, Widen, Never, Past, Answer, **and** Together)

20. Vital

21. I Before E

22. Premiere

23. Focus Group

24. Aimlessly

25. Thanks for the Memory

ABOUT OUR PUZZLERS

NANCY LINDE lives near Boston, Massachusetts. After more than twenty years as a documentary filmmaker, she started Never2Old4Games, a company that provides high-quality games, quizzes, and puzzles for professionals who work with seniors in group settings. She is also the author of *399 Games, Puzzles and Trivia Challenges Specially Designed to Keep Your Brain Young* (Workman Publishing, 2012), an exuberant collection of brain-exercising games. Nancy believes passionately in the power of games to enhance health and happiness at any age.

For more about Nancy's games for seniors, check out www.never2old4games.com.

DAVID HOYT is the self-confessed puzzled mind behind a long list of wildly popular games, puzzles, and brain teasers including Jumble™, Word Roundup™, Up & Down Words™, Word Winder™, and many other puzzles featured in more than 600 newspapers! Since the early 1990s, his passion for puzzles has grown into a full-time profession, and he feels very fortunate to have such a fun job. For this book in particular, he hopes you enjoy the puzzles he's put together for you, especially since a few are brand-new puzzle formats making their world debut!

COLIN MORGAN is an architect, puzzle writer, and game inventor. He grew up in the Pacific Northwest, spent a decade designing high rises in Chicago, and now divides his time between America and Europe, designing games full-time with his partner, David Hoyt.

To see more of David and Colin's work, check out: www.dlhoyt.com.

PATTI VAROL lives in Long Beach, California, where she makes crossword puzzles and word games instead of finishing her novel. She also roots for the Mets, tries to break video games, writes book reviews, teaches yoga, and cooks gourmet meals instead of finishing her novel. A freelance writer and editor, Patti is also crossword editor for Uptown Puzzle Club and assistant editor for the *L.A. Times* crossword.

For more of her puzzles, plus book reviews, stories, and essays, visit: www.pattivarol.com.

WIL ZAMBOLE is a freelance puzzle, event, and game designer for his startup company, Sightgags. He has written and edited trivia and puzzles (including puzzle hunts) that have appeared in magazines, websites, competitions, and even a mobile app. He has designed two long-standing events at Gen Con called Cardhalla and The Instant Game Show and a new trivia event called Furthest from the Truth. He knows that he would not be where he is without the great help and advice from designer Mike Selinker and the motivation and love that his wife, Kim, shows him every day.

NEED MORE?

TRY THESE OTHER BRAIN-BUILDING MARBLES PRODUCTS:

FIDDLESTICKS

These colorful wooden blocks can be manipulated into endless shapes and are great at teaching dexterity, problem solving, and color-recognition skills.

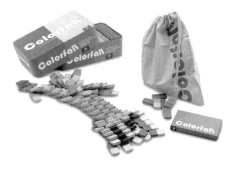

COLORFALL

Set up colored tiles according to the design card, then knock them down to reveal the image. Create 20 different designs with 200 colored tiles or free play with your own formations!

What it does for your brain: Exercises your visual processing, planning, spatial reasoning, and hand-eye coordination.

IDIOMADDICT

Decipher idioms and common phrases from clues read by the opposing team(s) to advance on the game board. Win or lose, you'll give your brain's language centers a workout. And the prize of a bigger brain is nothing to sneeze at!

What it does for your brain: Strengthens your word skills and memory recall speed.

ROCK ME ARCHIMEDES

Archimedes was a Greek mathematician, scientist, and all-around über-genius who discovered the laws of the level, which in playground terms is basically a teeter-totter. To win, just be the first player to oh-so-carefully get four marbles to your end of the board without reaching the tipping point, causing it to touch the table. **What it does for your brain:** Engages your parietal and frontal lobes with critical thinking and visual perception.

DA VINCI'S CATAPULT

Create a re-creation of Leonardo da Vinci's fifteenth-century catapult. With just over an hour of assembly time, this bad boy can hurl a small ball more than four meters, which comes in handy for ambushing pesky kid brothers or protecting cubicles from annoying coworkers. All pieces are precut and made with natural, untreated wood from sustainable forests. **What it does for your brain:** Uses your planning skills to build, and fine motor skills to construct.

MINDSTEIN

Work short-term and long-term memory with this challenging trivia party game. Answer five successive multiple-choice trivia questions on each turn. Letters correspond to correct answers, resulting in a five-letter word players race to shout. **What it does for your brain:** Activates your memory center and word-processing centers.